Dominick Murphy

Sketches of Irish Nunneries

First Series

Dominick Murphy

Sketches of Irish Nunneries
First Series

ISBN/EAN: 9783744740661

Printed in Europe, USA, Canada, Australia, Japan

Cover: Foto ©Andreas Hilbeck / pixelio.de

More available books at **www.hansebooks.com**

SKETCHES

OF

IRISH NUNNERIES.

WITH AN INTRODUCTION

ON

The Nature and Practice of a Conventual Life.

BY

THE REV. DOMINICK MURPHY,

DEAN, CORK.

FIRST SERIES.

DUBLIN:

JAMES DUFFY, 15, WELLINGTON-QUAY,

AND 22, PATERNOSTER-ROW, LONDON.

1865.

DUBLIN:
Printed by J. M. O'Toole & Son,
6 & 7, GREAT BRUNSWICK-ST.

PREFACE.

A CONSIDERABLE part of the matter contained in the following pages has been already before the public, and the rest has been in manuscript for a very long time. The Author intended that his sketches should extend to all the orders of religious women at present existing in this country, and he delayed their publication in the expectation that the pressure of his various duties would allow him to complete his original design. He has not, hitherto, succeeded in his wishes, and, rather than suppress altogether the matter he had prepared, he has determined to publish one Series, in the hope that, at some future time, he may be enabled to complete his work by the publication of another.

It is always a pleasing task to describe the holy lives and good works of those who devote themselves to God's service. The narration is a duty we owe to the good and holy for the virtues which they practise, and it is a benefit to the faithful at large, for it may encourage others to follow their example. When, moreover, the character of those holy women, who have made so great sacrifices for God, and who devote themselves with such heroic ardour to the service of the poor, is made the subject of discussion, and even of angry animadversion, in the high places of the land, it becomes a duty for all who know their worth to proclaim it to the world, and thus effectually repel the unjust and unmerited imputations that are directed against them. The suspicions with which the religious bodies are regarded in these countries, proceed more from ignorance than malice ; and the most effectual way to remove such suspicions is to explain, fully and accurately, what such bodies are, and what they are occupied in doing. Any one who is correctly acquainted with the nature of their state, and who has had an opportunity of seeing the magnitude and excellence of the labours in which they are engaged, cannot withhold from them his profoundest esteem and veneration. It is hoped that the following work, which describes a few of the religious orders now in active operation in this country, may tend to remove some of the prejudices which they still encounter, and place them before the world in the light in which they ought to be viewed. The world can ill afford to lose at any time, much less at present, the advantage of the light it receives from the example of the holy, the disinterested, the benevolent, and the good ; and, wherever that light is found, it should be put upon a candlestick, that it may shine on all the household, that all may see the good works, and give glory to their Father who is in heaven.

Cork, April 4, 1865.

INTRODUCTION

ON THE

NATURE AND PRACTICES OF THE RELIGIOUS LIFE.

THE history of those religious communities who have in
every age devoted themselves to the service of God, in the
different forms of monastic life, is a most interesting study for
the observant mind. In whatever light we view them, whether
as to the circumstances in which they had their origin, the
objects they proposed to themselves to accomplish, or the services which they did actually perform, they afford most abundant
and most profitable matter for reflection. Their annals bear the
same relation to the public records of the Church, that biography
does to general history. Each religious community possesses
an individual interest, and enjoys a separate and distinctive
character. We perceive it starting into existence; we watch
its progress to maturity; we contemplate it developing the
powers it possesses, and combating the influences by which
it is opposed; we admire the success or the renown it subsequently achieves, and often lament its final decay and
dissolution, and all with as much interest as we would
observe the life of a human being, or the several vicissitudes of
his history. And as the most interesting and instructive
passages in the life of any distinguished personage, are those
in which his character was formed, and the trials and struggles
in which his qualities were afterwards displayed, so will it
be found that the most interesting pages in the records of our
religious communities, are those of the founders, or their immediate successors, in which their distinctive character was formed,

B

or of critical periods of their existence, whether few or
many, whether isolated or continuous, when the passions of
wicked, or the power of misguided men, have been unscru-
pulously exerted against them. It is necessary to bear in mind,
that neither holiness nor usefulness will secure an exemption
from the injuries of wicked men. The world is often ungrateful
for services from which it has derived great benefit, and
frequently visits with obloquy virtues that should receive its
warmest approbation. In our own times, and even in our own
country, we see those dear and honoured communities, which
all know to be devoted, with the most untiring and single-
hearted zeal, to the sacred objects of religion and charity,
insulted by the most dishonouring insinuations, and often by the
foulest and most unsparing calumny. The same system is still
in use which was found successful in former times, that those
who have been previously robbed of their good name, may
be more easily and effectually despoiled of their influence and
their property. Independently of the interest which may be
taken in the history of the monastic bodies, every friend to
religion should endeavour to discharge his duty to them, by
paying the tribute of his homage to their spiritual excellence,
and by proposing to public consideration the nature of the
services which they render to society. Much of the injustice
that is done to the religious orders, springs more from ignorance
of their nature, than from any deliberate malice. It is to such
as are ignorant of the real nature of our religious community life,
or who have adopted, without suspicion, the misrepresentations of
its enemies, that many of the following observations are addressed.
To an honest inquirer, truth is always acceptable, however
much it may be at variance with his feelings or his prejudices;
and I hope that any one who bears with me patiently to the
end, will see ample reason to believe, that a religious community which devotes itself to the service of God in any of
the institutes authorized by the Church, and which carries
out the objects and spirit of its rule, is a source of Christian

edification and of social happiness, in whatever city or locality it is permanently established. This assertion applies to every religious community, whether of men or women. But on the present occasion it is to the religious communities of women, that our attention is to be exclusively directed.

A nun is a woman who consecrates herself to the especial service of God, by the vows of poverty, chastity, and obedience, and who leads a life of regular observance, according to the authorized rule of some religious community. A woman may make these vows without associating herself to others, and without entering a community, but she would not thus become a nun. The rule of life which they follow, should be sanctioned and proposed by the regular ecclesiastical authority, which, for the religious orders and congregations, must be that of the Holy See. The confirmation and final approval of every religious body, must come from the Supreme Pontiff, if it aspires to be permanent, or seeks to participate in the usual privileges. No one else has authority to confirm the erection of a new institute, or to sanction rules by which its members are to be permanently governed, according to the present and universal discipline of the Church.

Communities of women, living according to rule, and bound together by their vows, are of great antiquity in the Church. The example of monastic life, which was furnished to the early ages by the monks of Syria and Egypt, was not thrown away on the sex which has been always so keenly alive to the purer and holier impulses of grace, and so ready to respond to God's call in every path of virtue and perfection. Even in the life-time of the apostles, many women consecrated themselves to God by vow, though they lived at home in the bosom of their own families, surrounded by their friends. Circumstanced as the Christian world then was, convents, in the ordinary meaning of the word, were impossible; but in the third and fourth centuries, when, under the reign of Constantine and his successors, the profession of the Christian faith was no longer attended with danger, women began to form them-selves into communities, and to adopt the observance of a common rule. Saint Basil, in the fourth century, speaks expressly of convents, the inmates of which were subject to the direction of a superioress; and Saint Chrysostom says, that in his day the convents of women were nearly as numerous as those of men. There were, no doubt, many at the same time who adhered to the early practice of making their vows in the presence of the bishop, and living still with their own families. It is probable that these were recognized as re-ligious women by the Church and the people, and were also dressed in some distinctive apparel. But when convents began to be established, this mode of making vows and following the religious life, began gradually to get into disuse, and finally was altogether abandoned. The superior advantages of a com-munity over a solitary life, its greater security, its more abundant facilities of spiritual improvement, and its more decided edifying action on the faithful, made it prevail over the other; and all who wished to devote themselves to the religious life, usually entered one or other of such establishments. The members made a solemn profession of their state, put on a distinctive dress, and adopted a certain degree of enclosure or of seclusion from the world.

Saint Patrick introduced the observance of religious vows into Ireland, and recommended them to such of his converts as felt themselves called to a more perfect state of life. In the work called his " Confession," which has come down to our times, and the authenticity of which is not questioned, he says: " The sons of the Scots and the daughters of the petty kings, live like monks and virgins of Christ. There was even one Scottish lady, of blessed life and noble family, beautiful in person, and of adult age, whom I baptized. A few days after she came to me on a particular business. She had been advised, she said, by a messenger of God, to remain always a virgin of Christ, and that thus she would be nearer to God

Thanks be to God, on the sixth day after that she well and fervently took that course, which all the virgins of God do also; not always, however, with their parents' consent, who sometimes make them suffer both persecution and abuse on account of it. Nevertheless, the number is increasing every day; and we cannot count the number of those who are born to Christ of our race, besides those who are widows and live in continence."— *Confession*, 18.

It is probable that Saint Patrick did not require those who made vows to reside together. He had seen convents of women in Rome and in several parts of the Continent, but it was not until about ten or twelve years after his death that they were established in Ireland. It is natural to suppose that he frequently spoke of such a mode of life to his fellow-labourers in the ministry, and that he prepared the most fervent of his converts for its future adoption; but it was not until the year 490, when he had been some time dead, that his designs were carried into practical effect. The person who established the first nunnery was the celebrated Saint Brigid of Kildare. The circumstances of the foundation are worthy of being recorded. Her reputation for great virtue, and even for the possession of the gift of miracles, was spread far and wide. Great numbers of people came to her, attracted by the renown of her sanctity, to solicit her advice in their spiritual difficulties, and, perhaps, also to experience the benefit of that miraculous power which was popularly ascribed to her. As she was a native of the province of Leinster, and as her parents were persons of some consideration, her countrymen wished that the place of her birth should also be the place that should have the honour of her residence. They accordingly sent a deputation to solicit her return, and pledged themselves, at the same time, to provide her with suitable accommodation and sufficient means of subsistance. She complied with the request, and was welcomed most warmly. They assigned her and her companions a plot of ground, which was distinguished from all the surrounding country by a

large oak-tree which grew on the spot, and which, to merit
such a distinction in a country generally well-wooded, must
have been one of a gigantic size. Beneath the shade of its
gnarled and wide-spreading branches, they erected a convent
for the saint and her associates. The oak remained for many
a year, and gave shelter to many succeeding generations, and
also the name of Kildare to the monastery and church, and,
finally, to the town that gradually grew up around it. The
nuns lived on the produce of their land ; and as their wants
were few, it was sufficient. A strange custom of these nuns
was the preservation of a perpetual fire, of which no other
instance occurs. It began in the days of Saint Brigid, by her
direction, and continued in order that it should be a benefit to
the poor, and be ever ready to receive the cold, wet, and way-
worn stranger, who may present himself at their gates. The
hospitality of the Irish nation has been always acknowledged ;
but there is something exceedingly beautiful and touching in
thus placing it under the immediate sanction of religion, and
appointing its chosen servants to keep their sleepless watch over
that ever-burning fire, which, by night and day, in wet and
cold, was ever ready to receive the weary traveller, and give
shelter to those that stood in need. It was put out for a time
by Henry de Loundres, Archbishop of Dublin, in the year
1220, but was soon lighted again, and continued burning until
the final dissolution of monasteries, in the reign of Henry VIII.*

* Cambrensis gives the following account of the fire called *inextinguishable*,
in ancient times preserved at Kildare, by the nuns of Saint Brigid :—
"At Kildare, which the glorious Brigid renders illustrious, are many
miracles worthy of notice; and the first is, Saint Brigid's fire, called the
inextinguishable fire, not that it cannot be put out, but because the nuns
and religious persons are so careful and diligent in supplying it and recruiting
it with fuel, that from the time of that virgin it hath remained always unex-
tinguished through so many successions of years; and though so vast a
quantity of fuel hath been in such a length of time consumed in it, yet the
ashes never increased."
"But this fire was extinguished by Henry de Loundres, Archbishop of
Dublin, in 1220, as may be seen in an anonymous author of the Dominican
Order, who died in 1314. Perhaps the archbishop put out the fire because the

The order of Saint Brigid spread rapidly through the other provinces of the kingdom.   Their rule was very simple and primitive, consisting principally of prayer and manual labour, the instruction of the neighbouring poor in the truths and duties of religion, and the spiritual consolation of those who applied to them for the purpose.   All the nunneries of the order, wherever they were situated, were subject to the jurisdiction of the Abbess of Kildare, who also had the privilege of nominating the bishop of that diocese, whenever a vacancy occurred.

During the long period of nearly a thousand years, that elapsed from the time of Brigid to that of the suppression of convents, many changes must have taken place in the fortune and discipline of this institute, which are only vaguely indicated in the imperfect chronicles that have come down to our times.   Some of the convents were destroyed by the ravages of the Northmen; many were extinguished by those intestine wars which the Irish chieftains were ever waging with one another for some wretched cause, and from the disastrous consequences of which, neither the sanctity of God's house, nor the seclusion of the cloister, was able to protect their inmates.   The remainder, probably, exchanged their rule for the modern and more useful institutes that were being propagated in the Western Church.   We find mention in the annals of several flourishing convents of the Canonesses of Saint Augustine, of some of the Benedictines, and also of the Cistercians.   These are the only religious orders of women, whose establishment in Ireland, before the sixteenth century, we can look on as absolutely certain.

custom not being used in other places, it might seem to have taken its origin from an imitation of the Vestal Virgins, whom Numa Pompilius first instituted, and dedicated to the holy mysteries of Vesta, for the preservation of a perpetual fire.   Be that as it may, without doubt, this custom of preserving a fire in that convent by the nuns of Saint Brigid, for the benefit of the poor and stranger (as was pretended), was continued down to the suppression of monasteries, in the reign of Henry VIII."— *Ware's Antiquities*, vol. ii. page 238.

For a period of two centuries from the Reformation, the existence of the Catholic body in Ireland was a continuous struggle for the free and secure exercise of their religion. The religious orders were in a special manner an object of persecution, and received no indulgence from those who were in power. It is not to be expected, therefore, that many women would be found to encounter the dangers of a convent life. A few did so, and it will be seen how it fared with them. But it was only when a brighter era seemed dawning on their country, towards the close of the last century, that Catholics began to indulge the hope of being allowed to worship God in freedom and security, according to the dictates of their conscience, and of serving God according to whatever mode of life and rule of conduct they may deem most conducive to His honour and glory, and most beneficial to their brethren.

Having thus alluded, in a brief and imperfect manner, to the history of the few conventual institutions that existed in this country prior to the sixteenth century, and before we proceed to consider the brighter pages of their history in subsequent years, let us, for a moment, pause to consider what a nunnery really is. Many have most vague and indistinct ideas upon this subject; and many more have, not only vague ideas, but are labouring under most erroneous impressions, and entertain opinions absolutely at variance with the truth. Let us proceed to examine it minutely and in detail. The instant we enter a nunnery, we find that it is inhabited by a number of females, clothed in a uniform dress of some particular kind, which is different from what is now usually worn by persons of their age and sex. Such dress is the habit of their order. Nuns of that order, in every part of the world, wear that habit, and no other. Each order has its peculiar habit, which distinguishes it from every other, and is immediately recognized by persons having any experience or knowledge of the different religious bodies. It is very different from the costume worn at the present day, but it was once the costume worn by respectable females of the better classes of society. Fashion has drifted far, very far, indeed, away, but they have remained as they were, and still adhere to the plain and unadorned raiment which formed the apparel of holy women in the times that are gone. It will be admitted that its simplicity and sobriety effectually preserve them from the besetting weakness of their sex, and its grave and serious appearance well becomes those who have resolved to die to the world, and give themselves to God. Such as wear white veils on their heads are novices, who have not yet made their vows, and who are, therefore, only in preparation for the religious profession. When their training is complete, and it is to last for two years, they will be enrolled among the regular members of the community. Those others, who are engaged in the menial offices of the house, are called lay sisters. They make vows like the rest, with this only difference, that, while the others devote themselves to instruction, and the several works of charity, they devote themselves expressly to minister in the capacity of servants to the domestic wants of the other members of the community.

For the purposes of domestic government, and the due performance of the works of charity and religion to which they are expressly devoted, they constitute what may be termed a corporate body. The head which is to preside over it, is elected by the free and unbiassed suffrages of the members. They all know the character and the qualities of one another; they all have a direct personal interest in the result of their selection; they are, therefore, likely to choose for their superioress the person most capable of promoting the interests of all. Her authority expires after a period, which, in some orders, is limited to three, in others to six years. During the period of her administration, she is bound to exercise her power according to the rules and constitutions of her institute, which, when approved of by the Holy See, become the charter of the body, by which the superioress must exercise her authority, and all must regulate their lives. In all that relates to the objects of the institute, the

members are bound to obedience to the superioress in every
matter which does not involve the guilt of sin. It is scarcely
n cessary to observe, that there is no authority on this earth,
either civil or ecclesiastical, that can lawfully require or command the commission of even the smallest sin.

A little reflection will enable us to discover what, indeed, the
experience of all ages has abundantly confirmed, that no religious
community can be formed, or, if formed, can permanently hold
together, which is not bound together by religious obligations.
The fundamental principles of religious communities, which
have been sanctioned by the Catholic Church, and which have
been found effectual, are those of poverty, chastity, and obedience.
These obligations are self-imposed. The Church recognizes no
authority on this earth by which they can be imposed on any
one who does not feel called by the divine grace to contract
them. This is purely a matter between the individual soul and
God, and must be determined by such lights as the individual
may possess for the direction of the conscience. If the
individual comes to the conscientious conclusion that God does
not call to these sacrifices, they should not be made, and cannot
be required; but should the decision be otherwise, the person
who is docile to the inspirations of grace, ratifies and confirms
it by undertaking these serious obligations, and consecrating
that resolve by formal vow, which may be either private,
when made in some form or society not approved by the Holy
See for that purpose, or solemn and public, when it is made in
some recognized religious institute or order formally confirmed
by the Church. As these are contracted by every one who
embraces the conventual life by making religious vows, and as
they are the fundamental principles on which the conventual
life rests, it is necessary for the perfect understanding of the
subject that we consider them separately.

Poverty is the state or condition of one who has no earthly
goods in his possession, or at least who has no more than is
sufficient to afford him the bare necessaries of life. If a person

has no property, and can have none—if a person gives all that was ever possessed or enjoyed, and binds him or herself never to have any beyond the mere necessaries of life, that person is poor in the strictest sense of the word.   Such a one may hold property in trust for others, or may have a right to employ it for religious or charitable purposes, or may reside in a fine building, or may be never reduced to experience any of the bitter pinchings of destitution, having secured to them the necessaries of subsistence; but such a one must be looked on as, in truth, a poor person, in the most rigorous acceptation of the word. This individual poverty is united in convent life with a community of goods.   Whatever the members of a community enjoy of worldly goods, is possessed by them all in common; and the power of disposing or distributing these goods is vested in the superior elected or chosen according to their approved rules, and the property they seem to have is only held in trust, and should be applied to the purposes of the community at large.   No individual of that community can own anything, or dispose of anything, or look on anything as her own exclusive property, not even the dress she wears.   Each member has a right to receive whatever is necessary for the subsistence of the body, but having received food and clothing, with these, in the words of holy Scripture, she should be content, and can in strict justice claim no more. It will be seen at once, that poverty, taken in this sense, is necessary for every form of conventual life; for if individuals be permitted to have separate and distinct possessions, be they little or much, they must have separate interests.   Where there are distinct interests, there will necessarily be individual requirements, and provisions must be made to meet these requirements.   Some will have greater, some less stakes at issue in the prosperity of the body, and will consequently be more or less interested in its welfare.   The inconveniences of such a state of things may be easily conceived.   All individual claims and interests must yield to the common good; whatever they possess must belong to the body at large. When this disposal of worldly possessions is freely and voluntarily made, in order that, having divested themselves of worldly cares, they may be free to devote themselves to the service of God and of His poor, it is a sacrifice of great spiritual value. This voluntary poverty is not only a Christian virtue, but it is a perfection which, though not imperative on all, is yet of great merit in the sight of God, when embraced purely and disinterestedly for Him. I know that the very word poverty has a harsh and repulsive sound for men filled with the spirit of the world. I know that the substance which that word represents, is a thing which fills their souls with terror at its probable coming, and which haunts them in all their walks and moments, like a spectre, to their dying day. I know that it has sorrow and anxiety, and haggard misery and gaunt despair, following in its train through the dwellings of men, and carrying ruin and havoc into the proudest mansion that ever noble dwelt in, the instant it sets foot within its walls. I know all this, but I know also that the poverty which the world so dreads and shuns, has been made an excellence and a perfection of the Gospel. It is not merely that it furnishes occasions of practising patience and submission to the divine will, or of evincing one's own fidelity to duty in the manifold trials to which he may be exposed; but it has been so raised in its spiritual value, that those who voluntarily embrace it, and who become poor for Christ's sake, have a special blessing promised to them from above. When the young man, mentioned in the Gospel, said to our Lord, "What shall I do that I may have life everlasting?" He answered, "If thou wilt enter into life, keep the commandments." But he said, "All these have I kept from my youth." Jesus answered, "If thou wilt be perfect, sell all thou hast, and give to the poor, and come and follow Me." (Mat. xix. 16.) Here we perceive that even for those who have kept the commandments from their youth (and who does not feel that such is a rare and inestimable grace?), there is a greater perfection and a higher excellence to be attained by those who become poor of their own free will, for the love of God.   This poverty the apostles practised. Some of them had but little to abandon, yet what they had they left after them.   " We have left all things, and followed Thee." And this surely was the example which their divine Master gave them in His own life and conduct. The wealth of the universe belonged to Him. Mines of immeasurable depth of brightest gold lay hid in the yet unexplored bosom of the earth, and gems of purest lustre, each worth a monarch's ransom, sparkled unseen in the caverned depths of ocean, which all belonged to Him. He could have had them, and much more, by merely uttering the wish; but He would not do so, because He would rather be poor for our sakes, than be rich in their possession. And I need not tell you how He chose a poor virgin for His mother, and lived for thirty years in her company. I need not tell you of the crib of Bethlehem, nor of the hut of Nazareth, nor how He worked for His daily bread with the labour of His hands, nor how He lived during the years of His public mission on the alms of the faithful, and that, when the tax-gatherer called on Him, He had to work a miracle to procure a penny, and how from the cross He saw His clothes divided among His executioners, and died so poor that the winding-sheet in which His body was enveloped, and the sepulchre in which it was laid, were the alms of His disciples. You know all these, and knowing and believing them as you do, can easily understand how those who wish to follow in His footsteps, and show their love for Him, should, even though they had kept all the commandments from their youth, still long for something more, and become poor for His love.

Yet, it may be said that the sacrifice made by a person enter-ing a religious community, is not exactly a compliance with the recommendation made by our Lord to the young man in the Gospel. But it is surely some approach to it to give up all right to every temporal property beyond the mere necessaries of life, and to be able to say with truth, and in all sincerity, I do not wish to have, and I never shall have, any possession of my own.

I now abandon everything I have, be it much or little; everything I may be entitled to, as well as all I may hereafter expect to receive. I give up all for ever; and, having food and clothing of the simplest and most frugal kind, I shall be content with them, and shall not receive, nor have the power of receiving, any more during the period of my life, however much it may be prolonged.

This, surely, is a choice of voluntary poverty; and, when done for the purpose of devoting oneself to works of charity and religion, it is surely equivalent to selling all, and giving it to the poor. When, moreover, in addition to the renouncing of all goods actually possessed, a nun gives up for ever all that she may have a reasonable expectation of possessing, or which she may even have a legal right to possess at some time, perhaps not very remote, or which she may hope for from her youth, her position in society, her accomplishments, her gifts of nature or education, her family influence or connexions—surely such a sacrifice, made in all the fervour and sincerity of the heart, is equivalent to the voluntary poverty recommended to the young man in the Gospel. Nay, it is more than equivalent to it; for thus are fulfilled, in the spirit as well as the letter, the sublime sacrifices pointed out in the words of the Redeemer: "Amen, amen, I say unto you, every one that hath left house, or brethren, or sisters, or father, or mother, or wife, or children, or lands." This she does for Christ's sake, to be poor like Him, to devote herself to the service of the poor; and we can have no doubt but that the promise will also be fulfilled, and that the blessings consequent on such abandonment will, in their own good time, be also realized: "She shall receive an hundred-fold, and shall possess life everlasting."

If it be necessary that those who become members of a religious community should renounce all right to the possession or disposal of property, it must be admitted, also, that it is still more necessary for them to renounce all the ties of family; for, it can be seen that a person who has, or may have a family, whether husband, or wife, or children, can never become a truly earnest and devoted member. Wherever these members of a family exist, their claims must be paramount to all other human obligations. Any one who is fettered by them, can never really and earnestly be devoted to the objects of a religious institute; and if any considerable proportion of the members should have contracted such obligations, the body itself would soon, and inevitably, be dissolved. Hence the obligation of leading a single life during the period of connexion with the institute, becomes not only a matter of propriety, but of absolute necessity. As the period of connexion is usually, and with few exceptions, for life, so also should be the obligation of remaining single; and, in order that celibacy may be rendered more easy, more obligatory, and more meritorious, it should be undertaken under the sanction of religion, by a vow of chastity, either temporary, if the choice be made for only a few years, or perpetual, if the obligation be accepted for life.

The superior excellence of holy virginity, and the greater merit of a single life, when chosen for the honour and glory of God, above that of marriage, is so universally admitted among all Catholics, that it may seem unnecessary to point out to you the reasons which establish the truth of such an opinion; yet, as it is one on which much prejudice prevails, and great misunderstanding exists among those who differ from us in religious belief, it may not be altogether out of place to enter a little into the consideration of the question at issue between us.

Any one who dispassionately considers the language of Saint Paul on this matter, must admit that a single life, when selected from religious motives, is holier and more excellent than the married life. This is evidently the meaning of the words of the apostle, contained in the seventh chapter of his first epistle to the Corinthians: "He that giveth his virgin in marriage doth well, but he that giveth her not, doth better." And again, he says: "A woman is bound by the law as long as her husband liveth; but if her husband die, she is at liberty: let her marry whom she will, only in the Lord. But more blessed shall she be if she so remain according to my counsel, for I think I have the Spirit of the Lord." He explains the reason why it is better for her so to remain. It is, because "the unmarried woman and the virgin thinketh on the things of the Lord, that she may be holy in body and in spirit; but she that is married thinketh on the things of the world, how she may please her husband." This is not a commandment, observe, for he says: "I have no commandment of the Lord, but I give counsel;" and his counsel is, that those who are unmarried should so remain, that they may be at liberty to devote themselves to the Lord. This object it is that imparts its superior spiritual excellence to a single life; for, if persons remain unmarried, that they may be at greater liberty to devote themselves to the pleasures and interests of life, their state is not better than the married, nor is it even so good. But when they give themselves to God, and devote themselves to His service in the unmarried state, it is better that they should so remain; and should they consecrate themselves to His service by any solemn religious vow or obligation, it is imperative on them to so remain. To break that vow would be to break faith with God. Hence, St. Paul, though declaring the superior excellence of the unmarried state, was very cautious in the selection of those whom he admitted to the privilege of thus devoting themselves to God by special consecration. He advises Timothy: "The younger widows avoid, for when they have grown wanton in Christ, they will marry, having damnation, because they have made void their first faith." Their marriage, therefore, must be a violation of some faith that had been previously pledged; and must entail damnation, because it violated that faith. Why should this be so, if they, being widows, and still young, were at liberty to enter upon a second marriage? The marriage tie is utterly dissolved by the death of the husband, and a second marriage, in ordinary cases, has never been pronounced a sin. Why, then, should they, by marrying, incur the terrible guilt and penalty implied in the word damnation? Were they not at liberty to change their minds, and, when tired of widowhood, to enter again into the state of marriage, which the apostle had declared they may do only in the Lord? No; they were not at liberty to change their minds, if, by their deliberate choice, they had already chosen a life of celibacy for themselves; if they had consecrated their widowhood to God's service by a formal religious oblation, and if, of their own free will, they had pledged their faith to Him. There was no obligation on them to make that consecration. There were many who did not do so; but those who did, were obliged to make good that consecration. They could no longer retrace their steps. They had pledged their solemn faith, and they were obliged to keep it. If they were young and rich, and gifted and accomplished, and of good standing in the world, they may have had many temptations and inducements to reconsider their determination. But woe to them if they yielded to the seductions of flesh and blood, and broke the faith they had already pledged to God, and married. "They had damnation," says St. Paul, because they made void that faith, and for no other cause.

But is not " marriage honorable in all "? Yes, certainly it is, but only in those who enter that state without any lawful impediment. Nay, the Catholic Church honours marriage more than any Protestant community, for it claims for it the honour of a sacrament, and believes it to have been raised, from a mere religious and social contract, to the dignity of a sacrament of the New Law. Yet, though marriage is thus honorable, all admit that there may exist certain restrictions or impediments to prevent marriage from being at all times, or by all persons, indiscriminately contracted; and that if marriage be entered on in defiance of such lawful impediments, it is no longer honorable, but becomes a sin, perhaps an infamy—nay, sometimes a sacrilege. When we are told, therefore, that marriage is honorable in all, we must evidently understand this with several limitations. It is honorable in those who labour under no lawful impediment. Each individual has power to enter the married state, but each individual has also power to abstain, if he chooses to do so. Marriage will be the condition of the mass of the human race. But there are many who will never contract it, and who have a perfect right, from nature, from society, and from religion, to remain unmarried, if they think it expedient to do so. Every one who comes into the world has the power to exercise the right of choice, and to remain single if he pleases; and if he thinks, on coming to mature years and judgment, that a single life is preferable, that it is more excellent and meritorious in the sight of God, that it will enable him to devote his faculties of mind and body to the public good with more success, that it will permit him to make sacrifices of his worldly interests, which, if he were married, he would not be at liberty to make, has he not the fullest right to select it as his position, if he will? If, moreover, he desires to give his choice a religious sanction, to make it holier and more binding upon his conscience, and hopes to resist the fluctuations of the human will, and the temptations of human infirmities, by the solemn obligation of a promise or a vow to God, that promise is surely entitled to the strictest observance. Will any one say, that having in mature years, with full reflection and free choice, made that offering, he is then, at the first breath of passion, in the first moment of weakness, or on the first call of the meaner interests of the world, at liberty to change his mind, and fling to the winds the vow he has made, and the sacred obligation he has contracted? No; neither the Church nor society required of him to make it at first. He made it with his own free choice; but when once made, reason, religion, and the first principles of honour, require that it be kept, and its obligations be conscientiously fulfilled.

If you contemplate the examples preserved for us in the pages of the Gospel and the ecclesiastical history, you will find how exalted a place virginity and celibacy have ever held in the estimation of the most eminent servants of God. Our divine Lord had a pure and immaculate virgin for a mother; He had a virgin for His precursor; He had a virgin for His bosom friend; His apostles led lives of celibacy from the moment that He called them to His service. Those only who have been virgins to their dying hour, are worthy to sing that canticle of praise and adoration, which the enraptured apostle heard before the throne of the Lamb; and we may add, that though the married life is holy and sanctified by many graces, and adorned frequently with many virtues, yet it will be found that those who have most ardently given themselves to God's service, who have made the greatest sacrifices for God's people, who have devoted themselves with the most heroic constancy to every generous work of charity, and who have left the most enduring monuments of zeal and piety, have not been those who had wives, or husbands, or sons, or daughters, to divide their solicitude, but that these great works were done by holy men and women who left wife, and husband, and father, and mother, and every tie and hope of family, and gave themselves in holy celibacy to religion, charity, and God.

The third vow made by the members of a religious community is that of obedience. Though it comes third in the order of enumeration, it is in reality one of the most important. Indeed, in some of the religious bodies, it is made to include all the others. The necessity of obedience in all forms of community life is obvious to every one. No body of persons can combine for a common object, without giving up much of their own will; and the more of their own will they are prevailed on to give up, the greater will be the unity, and consequently the efficiency, of their common action. Hence we perceive that in those bodies where the most complete unity and efficiency of action is required, the head is invested with an almost despotic authority. I need only mention, for example sake, the case of an army, where the commander is usually invested with such power, that no order he issues, however strange, will admit of being questioned, or however difficult will admit of being disobeyed. The members of a religious community are not, indeed, bound to such entire and unquestioning obedience as is exacted in military service; but as they are combined for the attainment of a common object, their will and inclination must be rendered subservient to the attainment of that object, and their united action can only be secured for that purpose by the supremacy of some one individual, who is invested with the necessary authority to direct, to control, to command, and to insist on, if necessary, the observance of such commands as may be issued. This authority implies, as a necessary consequence, the corresponding obligation of obedience on the part of those who are subject to that authority.

Every Christian acknowledges that obedience is a virtue which forms the basis of all moral duty. In fact, the entire system of moral and religious obligation presupposes the excellence of humble obedience. The service of God implies obedience; our duty to parents, pastors, masters, superiors, spiritual and temporal, ceases to be such unless we admit the merit of obedience. But in these departments of duty, obedience is a virtue which we are bound to practise, and which we cannot refuse without the guilt of sin; but it is a virtue, too, which, in our several departments of religious duty, is required of all, without any exception. And should we voluntarily place ourselves in subjection to those who have no authority save what is given by our own act, should we place ourselves under their direction, and bind ourselves to be obedient to their commands in those matters where God's will is not otherwise made known to us, we practise an obedience beyond what the great body of Christians are bound to practise. We make a sacrifice of our will, more perfect and more extensive than others are bound in strict duty to do; and when this is done for the sake of pleasing God, for the more perfect practice of virtue, for the more thoroughly and efficiently promoting the glory of God or the welfare of our neighbour, it becomes a perfection of the Gospel virtue, which, though not obligatory on all, still may be practised with much benefit. Such voluntary obedience has a greater intrinsic excellence than ordinary obedience, which it' not only includes but surpasses, and makes those who practise it, from a spirit of pure religious sacrifice, more like that great and perfect Being who, though He was God and King of all, yet humbled Himself, and became obedient even to death, and was subject to Joseph and Mary with the docility of a little child, and did their bidding in all things, and even worked for them at a trade, though He was the King of all.

It may be objected, perhaps, that there is danger of abuse in such an obligation of obedience; that a person who makes such a vow may be required to do something wrong, or sinful, or displeasing to God. But all know and recognize the principle of Christian duty, that God's commands must be supreme over all others, and that no authority on this earth, ecclesiastical or civil, has any right to set His commands aside, and authorize the commission of even the smallest sin. The obligation of obedience arising from a religious vow, can, therefore, only extend to those things in which we are left at liberty by him; and that if any one be required to do what is sinful or wicked, such a command, if we may suppose it issued, must be disobeyed, and such disobedience would become a conscientious obligation. There can, therefore, be no room for such an objection as this in our system of religious discipline.

Again it may be objected to the system of religious obedience, that it argues great weakness of character thus to place ourselves to such an extent in the power of others, as to be bound by the most sacred of ties to do their bidding for a considerable time, nay, perhaps, for life. But, besides the necessity of such submission, when persons have combined for a common purpose, it is not unfrequently one of the most salutary spiritual exercises which persons can perform. It is particularly salutary to those—and there are many such—who labour under the disadvantage of a proud, conceited, selfish, and stubborn disposition. A person of this character may not find it easy, or, perhaps, may not see the advantage of submitting will and judgment to the guidance of others, however enlightened and dispassionate; but the greater the difficulty experienced, the greater will be the necessity for doing so. If a person of this kind submits to a course of judicious mental training, one of the first lessons to be learned, and one of the most essential to be practised, must be, that a distrust of one's own powers, and a docility to the suggestions of others, are ingredients in the formation of every perfect character, and that humility and obedience are the foundations of the real, and especially of all exalted virtue.

When, moreover, we reflect on the weakness, the instability, the irresolution of many who are sincerely disposed to do good, and how few have the knowledge to direct their powers and talents to the object of their lives, and, at the same time, the energy to command their constant and systematic exercise, or, in other words, how few are qualified to be their own masters, we must admit that it would be well for many to be constantly under the guidance of some one whose authority they would be made to feel, and in whose judgment they could place full confidence. How much of precious time is lost, of great powers frittered away, and of valuable lives doomed to unprofitable sterility, because persons have not been able to make up their minds as to what they should do, or how or when to do it! How much of great talent remains idle and unprofitable, because the possessors have not energy of mind enough to employ it at the proper time, or in the proper manner! There are very few, indeed, who do not feel that life would be more usefully and meritoriously spent, if it had been always directed by a prudent and skilful superior, who would not only be able to guide, but would also have such authority as would enforce the observance of his commands. If the full capability of our nature is to be developed, and continuously exerted, it is thus it is to be done. If the proverbial inconstancy of the human will is to be corrected, and that most important but wayward faculty to be kept in order, and exerted for good, it can be best done by subjecting it to the salutary restraints of holy obedience. Without this, it will be in danger of drifting helplessly before every wind of passion, like a ship without a rudder, and end by consigning the noblest powers of mind, and the greatest gifts of fortune, to certain and inevitable destruction.

These three virtues, as now described, are what are known as the evangelical perfections. They are not of general obligation on all Christians, but are counselled to those who have grace and strength to practise them. Some, or all of them, may be observed by persons in the world who are not living in any religious community, and who are not distinguished by any external dress or emblem, and are content to be seen and known by God alone, and by their spiritual director. Such persons, holy as they may be, are but isolated and solitary instances of that perfection which, in convents, is practised in a regular, combined, and systematic manner. The practice of these virtues is not there left to individual piety, but it becomes the business of a profession. The religious state has this object primarily in view, and the rules and observances of every institute are methodically arranged with reference to its accomplishment. A person who practises these virtues in a private condition, may fall away from the fervour once felt, and altogether omit their observance, without becoming liable to any charge of having changed a state of life, or abandoned a profession. But it is quite different with respect to a member of a religious community. The fundamental principle on which the existence of such a state of life depends, is the systematic observance of these evangelical counsels; and when these are given up, the state of life is essentially altered, and the profession of a religious is altogether abandoned.

Here let us pause for a moment or two, to consider what is usually meant by the excellence of a state of life. Some suppose that the state of life is most excellent which furnishes the most occasions of supernatural merit, and which conducts to the most abundant reward in a future condition of existence. But it is neither the degree of supernatural merit of its duties, nor the abundance of the reward which will be the consequence of their due performance, that determines this intrinsic excellence; for, we believe that some persons in the married state, and in the busiest occupations of the world, will be higher and happier in heaven than many members even of the most rigorous and contemplative institutes, though we believe, at the same time, that the latter state of life is more excellent than the former. Many, again, suppose that a generous and heroic performance of the corporal works of mercy, and a life of disinterested self-devotion, to promote the happiness or mitigate the misery of our neighbour, is the noblest sphere of duty, and that the tribute of admiration which it invariably and infallibly commands, is decisive of the question; and every one must, indeed, admit, that in certain conditions of society, certain critical circum-stances of time, or afflicting visitations of humanity, such an exercise of charity should claim precedence of all others, and be, at the same time, more conducive to the divine glory, and more obligatory on ourselves. But, in the ordinary condition of our existence, it is easy to conceive that the state of life which approximates most nearly to the condition of existence which we have been created to enjoy, and which also prepares us most directly and securely for that future destiny, and which realizes here on earth, as far as the imperfections of nature will allow, the exercise and occupation of that future state, must be intrinsically the most excellent; and, as the final condition of our existence is to be one of contemplation of the divine nature, of worship of His increated majesty, and of adoration of His infinite goodness, so the state which realizes, as far as possible, these heavenly functions, must be intrinsically and essentially the noblest exercise of our faculties, and the highest condition of our earthly existence. No one will assert that a work of mercy to the poor, such as feeding the hungry, or visiting the sick, though it may at times take precedence, and be more immediately obligatory, as to its performance, is so intrinsically excellent as an act of prayer or worship. When the question was raised by Martha, in the Gospel, our divine Lord, whose decision must be considered final, at once declared, that Mary, in whom the contemplative spirit was embodied, had chosen the better part; yet, though we must admit that the contemplative is more intrinsically noble than the active life, the latter may be, and often is, more conducive to the promotion of God's glory, appeals more strongly to the Christian sympathies, and may be attended by a more-abundant reward. Such are, probably, its claims in the present condition of society. When the poor, the suffering, and the ignorant, surround us on every side, and when the disastrous ravages of sin are spread so widely before our eyes, the generous Christian can have no doubt as to the path of perfection to be practically pursued. Though it may be more excellent to sit, like Magdalen, at the feet of our blessed Lord, and to speak to Him in holy prayer and adoration, and to listen with willing ears to those sweet words which He may address to the heart in His moments of blessed inspiration, and to have no care or thought but of Him and for Him; yet we know, also, that He has left us, as a legacy of His tenderness, the poor, the suffering, the ignorant, and the sorrowful, and that we must see Him, and minister to Him in their persons. "Whatever you do to these, my least brethren, you do unto Me." In our country, especially, with the great mass of poverty and ignorance that surrounds us, and the many spiritual and corporal necessities under which our people labour, we may be sure that the generous Christian soul that loves God best, will be also the one to devote itself most ardently and strenuously to the spiritual and corporal works of mercy.

Besides these essential obligations of poverty, chastity, and obedience, most communities of religious persons make a fourth vow, which has reference to and includes a special devotion to the objects for which the order is instituted. Thus, in the old

c

Order of Mercy for the Redemption of Captives, the members made the heroic vow of offering themselves as substitutes for those that were taken captive, if they should not have the means sufficient for their ransom.   Some of our modern institutes devoted themselves, by special vow, to the education of the poor, some to the visitation of the sick and infirm, and all to some special work of mercy.   These vows are made in the presence of the bishop or his deputy, under the solemn sanction of religion.   In most congregations they are to bind for life, and constitute a solemn compact, by which the person who makes them gives herself to God, and God, by the authority of His Church, receives her, and imparts to the offering His approval and sanction.   The person who makes that compact is no longer at liberty to go back to the state which she freely abandoned.

It may be said, as it has often been said, that vows which may not be broken during the long period of life, and engagements that are thus irrevocably made, are scarcely suited to the nature of human beings constituted as we are; and that, in fact, it is not fit or proper that persons should thus bind themselves by solemn religious ties which are never to be dissolved.   But is that always admitted to be true?   Are not the obligations of the marriage state holy and irrevocable?   Is not the compact made in marriage to last for the full term of life?   Is it not to outlive the affection, the sentiment, or the interest, in which it originated?   Can it be dissolved by any authority on this earth? It is indeed the act of a moment, and the ceremony but one of a few words, yet the bond it imposes on the married pair can be burst asunder by no power in this world.*   They may have entered the married state with but little reflection, with the most imperfect motives, or with the most uncongenial dispositions; yet no amount of subsequent evil or unhappiness will

---

* We say this in despite of all the powers which the Divorce Court or the law which created it can command.

warrant the dissolving of. that tie, which was imposed in the presence of God's altar by the sacred ceremony of marriage. And if a woman is justified in thus giving herself for life to her husband, and leaving father and mother, as she is bound to do, and cleaving to him, as the holy Scripture says, as the bone of his bone and the flesh of his flesh; whatever may prove the intrinsic worthlessness of the object of her young affections or the unhappiness of her after life, why should it not be proper or lawful for her to consecrate herself to God's service by vows not more irrevocable, and by obligations not more solemn, if, on mature deliberation, she thinks herself equal to the fulfilment of them, and that God has, by a particular suggestion of His grace, called her to adopt them.

But is there no danger that she may mistake her vocation, be subjected to undue influence, or regret, when too late, the obligations she contracted? I do not mean to assert that any of these things is actually impossible, because no institution in this world, however sublime or holy, is exempt from occasional abuse. The holiest institutions may be profaned, and the very sacraments themselves abused; but that abuse furnishes no argument against their excellence. But though we admit that such things may have occurred in the religious state, to whom is the evil to be attributed, or who are responsible for the lamentable results that have occurred? Surely religion is not responsible if it takes sufficient precautions that no undue influences be brought to bear on the candidates for admission, and that no one be admitted without having had ample time for consideration, as well as ample knowledge of the state of life which is about to be embraced. In order that we may see whether such be the case, let us examine the course usually pursued by those who wish to enter a religious community. Many, no doubt, think, that for the most part it originates in some girlish whim, caught up in some moment of enthusiasm, or perhaps insidiously suggested to some unthinking mind for mere interested purposes; that the young lady then leaves her parent's or guardian's house aga'nst their will, or perhaps without letting them know anything about it; goes to a convent, is received by the nuns, gets the veil, and makes her vows, in such rapid succession, that she is neither allowed to know her own mind, or the nature of the obligations she contracts, until some fine morning she finds herself bound irrevocably to a state of life which neither conscience nor public opinion will ever after permit her to abandon. There are several who think that such is the course invariably pursued, and such its inevitable consequences, and who will be exceedingly surprised and, perhaps, a little incredulous, when they are told in what manner the business is actually done.

In the first place, no one can make a solemn religious vow without having come to years of mature understanding. The Church requires a greater age for religious profession than is required by the legislature for entrance into the marriage state. The Council of Trent* makes null and void all solemn vows made before the person has entered on the seventeenth year of her age.

Secondly.—It is a maxim of the Catholic Church, put forward prominently in every book that treats of the spiritual life, that none should enter the religious state without having good reason to believe in conscience that God has called them to it. This call is to be no sudden burst of enthusiasm or fervour, which is always to be distrusted, but a settled conviction come to in the mind, after earnest prayer, diligent reflection, cool examination, consultation with intelligent friends and disinterested advisers—in a word, without employing all the means which prudence can suggest for arriving at a right and safe conclusion in the most important step in life, and, above all, having the sanction of the director, who is acquainted with the spiritual

---

* Professio non fiat ante decimum sextum annum expletum. Professio autem antea facta sit nulla, nullamque inducat obligationem ad alicujus Regulæ vel Religionis vel ordinis observationem aut alios quoscumque effectus.— *Conc. Trid.* Sess. 25.

state, and to whom they have made known the secret wishes and aspirations of their soul.

Thirdly.—The final resolution, once arrived at (and it may take years of examination before it be arrived at), should be communicated to family and friends; for in such an important matter as the choice of a state of life, they have a right to be made acquainted with it. It has to be canvassed, discussed, and, perhaps, opposed. It may be, for many a long month or year, stubbornly and steadfastly resisted. When it is at length acceded to, which will be, in several instances, very reluctantly, domestic arrangements have to be made, sundry expenses incurred, and long family consultations to be held, before the young lady reaches at last the haven of her hopes, and enters the portals of a convent.

Fourthly.—On entering the convent of her selection, she has to remain a period of four or five months a postulant—that is, a candidate trying still more her own disposition, and making herself practically acquainted with the nature of the state to which she aspires, before she formally contracts any of its obligations.

Fifthly.—At the expiration of that period, the ceremony of reception takes place. She now receives the religious habit, and is formally enrolled among the members of the community. Even after being thus enrolled in the community, she is not yet bound by any of its special obligations; she is still at perfect liberty to retire if she thinks proper. She commits no sin by doing so, if she change her mind, and will incur neither social stigma nor ecclesiastical censure. During this period of probation, she has a perfect opportunity of knowing every minute detail of her daily duties, of trying the steadiness of her own resolution, and of practically testing her physical and moral powers of endurance. This term of noviciate, which is not usually less than two years, and is often considerably more, affords full time to ascertain the sincerity of her vocation. If there be any mere sentimental impulse at work

c 2

upon her mind, or any mere fervour of enthusiasm influencing her character, it has full time to die out, and be extinguished before then. Should there have been any error as to the real nature of a convent life, or any poetical or ideal colouring in the picture formed in the youthful mind, or any ignorance of its actual working, they must be all thoroughly dissipated or corrected by the experience of that time. If, when all these opportunities have been afforded of becoming acquainted with the nature of conventual life, she perseveres in her determination, she is admitted at the close of the noviciate to make her final religious profession. Then only is she permitted to make her vows. It may be thought that all reasonable precautions have been thus taken, and, that by all these wise delays, every chance of abuse has been thoroughly eliminated; but the far-seeing solicitude of the Church is not yet exhausted, for there is finally, and—

Sixthly.—The examination before profession.

Lest there should be any influences employed to mislead her judgment, or to control her will, the Church provides that a person deputed by itself, and invested with all necessary authority, obtains an interview with the candidate for profession. Neither an inmate of the convent nor a member of her own family are permitted to be present at this interview. Her real wishes and sentiments are then ascertained, and she is formally interrogated whether it be with her own free choice she determines to present herself to make her final and solemn vows of religion. It is only when she has fully satisfied the person so appointed that it is her own free choice and firm determination, and has affixed her seal and signature to a written declaration to that effect, that she is allowed to proceed to the final completion of her purpose. It will seem that this office is one of a most important nature. It involves a sacred trust, and should be only confided to one who is above all suspicion, and whose character and disinterestedness should be a sufficient guarantee for its impartial exercise.

As no one is professed without undergoing this examination, you may be naturally anxious to know where the individual can be found so enlightened, so honest, so prudent, so disinterested, as to be fully qualified for this important office; and when I tell you that this office is entrusted by the Church to the ordinary of the diocese in which the convent is situated, and that he is required, in fullest exercise of his wisdom and episcopal authority, to see justice done, and that no undue influences are employed, I think you will admit, that in no better or safer hands could that sacred trust be possibly committed. If with all these precautions, and despite all these safeguards, persons are found who enter the religious state without knowing their own minds, or who have not proper vocations, or through worldly or interested motives, all we can say is, that they have no one to blame but themselves. Sufficient, and more than sufficient means have been provided by the maternal solicitude of the Church, for their protection. There is no other state or profession which has been rendered so secure from any possible danger of abuse; and we may say this also with truth, that if the candidates for the married state were to have a two-years' trial of each others temper and character, that but comparatively few would be found willing to enter, of their own free choice, into the final and irrevocable compact, and to take each other for man and wife for ever.

Persons who know little, and have had no experience of the lives of monks and nuns, are frequently under the impression that they lead a very idle and indolent existence. In the literature of Protestant countries, the very name has become synonymous with an idle, lazy, and good-for-nothing person. It was on this plea that the property they once held was taken from them, and handed over to the ladies and gentlemen by whom it is now possessed, and whose mental or bodily activity is not calculated to put to shame those whom they dispossessed, and whose labours for the public welfare are, for the most part, not of a very remarkable description. No one who knew

the details of the daily life of a nun, could say with truth that
her life was a lazy or an idle one. Let us see of what sort it is.
The first instance she gives of laziness is, that she gets up at
five o'clock in the morning, unless prevented by age, sickness,
or infirmity. After rising, she spends half or three-quarters of
an hour in prayer, and meditation on the truths and duties of
religion. Persons who are not acquainted with the nature of this
devotional exercise, may think that it is very easy; but it implies
a laborious intellectual process, which becomes easy only to those
who have long practised it, or who have received a special
gift of prayer from God. At seven there is Mass and communion, with the preparation before and thanksgiving after.
The frugal breakfast is no sooner over, than their presence is
required in their schools, hospitals, orphanages, or whatever be
the special work in which they are engaged. In their schools,
they are surrounded by little ones, and have their hands full
of work, and, with a short interval of recreation, are busily
employed until three or four o'clock in the afternoon. The
evening is divided between their religious exercises and their
studies, until at ten o'clock they retire, weary and exhausted, to
their beds, and begin next morning the same unvarying round
of prayer and occupation as before. Any one who says that
a life of this description—and it is the life of every religious
woman in these countries—is one of idleness and unprofitable
indolence, is either a wilful calumniator, or, which is more
probable, repeats the reckless assertions of others, without
attending to the meaning of his words.

But if not idle, it may be asked, whether such a life be not,
at least, comparatively unprofitable? Would they not do the
same amount of good if they were to remain at home, and
attend to the interests of their own families? Do we not see
every day ladies in every walk of social life, both married and
single, going about among the poor and sick, managing schools,
visiting public institutions, and doing a great deal of good in
their respective neighbourhoods? No doubt there are such

persons in every Christian community. I am very far from saying, that Christian charity and philanthropy are confined to the precincts of the cloister. There will always be kind and generous persons, with hearts overflowing with compassion for every form of human suffering ; but how few of them will be found to make the pursuit of Christian charity the great business of their lives! How few will give to it any of their time, or attention, or means, beyond what they can conveniently spare from the claims of their families, to whom their primary cares are due! The claims of the poor can be but secondary, and can only receive such attention as may be possible after the prior ones have been discharged. There is a vast difference between the person who merely does this, and that other who generously and heroically makes the poor the primary object of her care; who gives up home and family to devote herself to their necessities; who does this, not in a fit of devotional feeling, which may soon evaporate, or of temporary excitement, which soon subsides, but who takes up the interests of the poor as the great business of her life; and that she may do it the better and the more thoroughly, makes it the peculiar study of her profession; who is not waiting until the intervals of other duties allow of some spare time which may be devoted to the purpose, but who is always at her post, surrounded with all the appliances of relief to help the destitute, to comfort the afflicted, to visit the sick, to protect the orphan, to teach the ignorant; who is ready at all times and circumstances, and prepared at every moment and emergency, and ever watching upon the highway of human life, to pour the balm of consolation on the weary and the worn wayfarer, and to feed, and clothe, and shelter, and teach the outcast who may come in her way. Between these two departments of charity, there is a very wide interval, and an essential difference; and, notwithstanding the many noble examples of philanthropy that have been occasionally given by persons in worldly stations, and even of religious persuasions different from ours, whose claims upon our admiration we admit to the full, it is the woman that devotes herself exclusively and entirely to the work of charity that has the best claim upon society, and that should hold the highest place in the public estimation. When we hear of Mrs. Fry visiting the dark and fetid recesses of the prison, or of Miss Nightingale going to comfort and relieve the wounded soldier in a distant land, we give them gladly the tribute of applause which they richly deserve, and shall hold their names in honoured remembrance as an example to future times. But how few of their class have followed in their footsteps! Have not hundreds of the members of our religious communities done as much, or more?   Are they not all ready to brave the dangers of pestilence and death, and bound to cling to their posts, even though others should abandon it in lassitude, or be driven from it by fear?   The nun who spends her life in a crowded school, or in the wards of an hospital—who knows every hovel and lane for miles around her convent—who can call their inmates by name, and is familiar with their wants—who has been a friend to them in their necessities—she is surely a greater benefactor to her people than any mere occasional volunteer or amateur in the work of charity can possibly be. If ever a great work of public charity or extended usefulness is to be accomplished, and efficiently conducted, it will be done best under her care, and by her agency. The following pages will show with what signal success the great departments of public charity have been administered by religious communities in Ireland, and what great fruits have resulted from their labours. They are our real benefactors; and if their value was to be estimated by the standard of real excellence, their services would be inscribed in golden letters in the annals of their people. Instead of un-called-for legislative interference, or insulting insinuations of parliamentary enactment, the public would extend their means of usefulness, confide to their care many of those institutions which they alone can render truly efficient, and give them the sphere of a more abundant charity.

But there is another and powerful influence which nuns exercise on the world, and that is, the influence of their example. The contemplation of exalted virtue acts almost insensibly upon the mind. To see, to admire, to endeavour to imitate, are the several steps of the process which takes place within us. We live in a world of great distractions, and, without using harsher language, a world in which we are exposed to a great many corrupting influences. We are each day liable to be infected by the prevailing spirit of sensuality and worldliness, to which we are already so strongly predisposed. There is surely something needed to counteract this influence, and to neutralize the infection to which we are liable. The Christian can dispense with no means of resisting the poison which pervades the atmosphere in which he lives, or which tends to elevate his thoughts and sentiments above the sordid considerations of his earthly condition. This earth holds him very firmly in its grasp. It tries to engross his attention to the exclusion of everything else, and to absorb his every desire, so that none should remain for the higher interests of his being. The corruption of his nature exerts all its force to make him look on this earth, and see and think of nothing above. Whatever tends to weaken the ties that bind down his heart to the material interests of his being, or to elevate his thoughts to Christian perfection, or to excite within his breast an admiration, a love, a desire of the higher virtues, or to stimulate his zeal to the higher pursuits of the spiritual world, is surely a service of great value. Such is the example of those who devote themselves to the service of God in the religious state. Their obligations, well and faithfully discharged, of poverty, chastity, obedience, are a salutary lesson to the concupiscence of the flesh, the concupiscence of the eyes, and the pride of life; and their charity to the poor, boundless and devoted as it is, is a warning to the selfish and the worldly. Here is an excellence, not merely ideal and theoretical, such as may be read of in books, or heard of in distant lands, or flourishing in remote times, but here actually existing among ourselves, which we can see with our own eyes, and know to be attainable in this present world, and despite all its corrupting influences. There is something so beautiful, so holy, so sublime, in the character of a religious woman consecrated to God, that the world is forced to give her the tribute of its homage, and to admit, in despite even of the deepest religious prejudices, the holiness and grandeur of the position she occupies. Her hands are full of work, but she is labouring for the poor. Her heart is inflamed with charity, but it is for the wretched, the ignorant, and the sorrowful. Her soul is kindled with the holiest aspirations, but they are for the reign of God among men, and for her own union for ever with Him. " It would be idle to object," says the author of Thorndale, " that if all were to retreat into a life of celibacy, there would be soon no living world to retreat from. All men, we know, will not adopt, nor feel the least disposition to adopt, any such mode of existence. If a few choose to live apart thus, and to set in many things a peculiarly high example to the rest of mankind, they are doing a good service to the world. Very praiseworthy is the active navigator: he comes, and goes, and brings the treasures of all climes together; but he who keeps the beacon-light upon the hill—he, too, is at his post."

SKETCHES

OF

IRISH NUNNERIES.

DOMINICANS.

In considering the state and reviewing the history of the religious establishments of the kingdom, we must naturally give precedence to those which were introduced amongst us when Ireland was a more Catholic and a happier country than it subsequently became. We pass over those who had convents at one period, and who have since passed away—such as the Augustinian and Benedictine nuns, and commence with those of the Dominican order, who came to Ireland at a very early period, and who still continue to flourish amongst us. It is exceedingly probable that communities of Dominican nuns were introduced into this country at a very early period of their history, though the exact localities in which they were established cannot be now ascertained with accuracy. The learned author of the Hibernia Dominicana can only guess at their probable existence in the towns of Drogheda and Waterford, but it is morally certain that several others existed in various parts of the kingdom, of which the names have not been preserved, and whose site, or whose ruins, if they exist, cannot be now, at this distance of time, identified. About the close of the sixteenth

D

and the beginning of the following century, we begin to see our way more clearly. We know that in the year 1644 a community of Dominican nuns, under the title of Jesus and Mary, was established in Galway, and confirmed a few years afterwards by the Papal legate, Rinuccini. Among other conditions imposed, he directed that they should recite each day the Rosary of the Blessed Virgin Mary, to solicit from the divine mercy aid and protection for the afflicted Catholics of Ireland, in the dangers to which they were exposed in that most critical period of their history. On the taking of Galway, by Cromwell, in 1652, they were dispersed, and compelled to seek safety in flight. Many of them, along with members of other convents, sought refuge in Spain, where the poor fugitives found a most hospitable reception from the members of their respective orders. Of the Dominicans who fled from the sword of Cromwell, only two ever returned, and these were Sister Juliana Nolan and Sister Maria Lynch. When James II. ascended the throne of England, and more peaceful days seemed dawning on the Catholics of Ireland, it was deemed advisable to try and restore their former community. These two ladies were accordingly directed to return from Spain, and take up their residence in Galway. They succeeded in doing so in the year 1686. A house was taken for the purpose of a convent in the centre of the town, and they being joined by several novices, commenced without delay the daily exercises of the religious life, adopted strict enclosure, and had sufficient confidence in their stability to put on the habit of their order.

This calm was but the lull of the storm. Disastrous times came on, and the flattering prospects they so confidently indulged were soon destroyed. In the year 1697, the seventh of the reign of William III., an Act was passed by the Irish Parliament, having for its object the total suppression of the Catholic religion in Ireland. The ascendancy party had overcome all opposition, and they were resolved to exert their power to the utmost. They were determined to leave nothing undone

to root out of the Irish so^{il} the Church which had been the object of their bitterest enmity. Besides banishing every prelate
and dignitary under the severest penalties, they took the most
effectual measures they could for the suppression of all monasteries, nunneries, congregations, and all religious establishments,
of whatever style and title. Justices of the peace throughout
the kingdom were commanded to use their most strenuous exertions to carry this measure into execution. The convent of
Galway, though in the centre of a Catholic town, was not able
to escape. On the day before the feast of the Holy Apostles
Peter and Paul, it was visited by the officials of the government, the grate which guarded the enclosure rudely torn down,
and they themselves commanded to put off the religious habit,
and exchange it for the secular dress. " It was a melancholy
thing," says an eye-witness, O'Heyne, " to see the affliction of
our dear sisters, which was so great that even some of the Protestants themselves were moved to compassion. The sisters had
remained together in enclosure to the very last day fixed by the
authorities for their final dispersion, and as the fathers who
formed our community in Galway had all left for France on the
20th of March, there was no one to officiate for them after their
departure. Hence, besides other privations, they had to be
without Mass even on Sunday. I was then in the neighbourhood, engaged in preaching and hearing confessions (for that year
the clergy of the several parishes had to employ greater expedition
than at other times, on account of the paucity of priests), and
when I heard of this circumstance, and of the lamentable state
in which they were, I came at once and officiated for them from
the 10th of April until the 17th of June, on which day I had
to go on board ship with one hundred and twenty-six religious
of other orders, who had to leave the country."

These are the words in which O'Heyne, a Dominican father
of the community of Galway, describes their lamentable condition. On the 29th of June the convent was closed. The nuns

dispersed; some sought shelter in the houses of their friends and relatives; others obtained a livelihood by manual labour in some industrial occupation. The house they occupied was taken possession of by the Government, and became a barracks for a company of soldiers.

In the year 1717, the Provincial of the Dominicans being on his visitation in Galway, and seeing the wretched condition of the nuns then living, who, for the most part, were scattered about among their friends, apparently with little hope of being restored to their convent, applied to the Archbishop of Dublin to receive some of them into his diocese. It was found that within the very shadow of the Castle of Dublin, and in the immediate vicinity of the Government, there was more safety than at a distance from the capital. The Archbishop having given a favourable answer to the application, eight nuns were directed to proceed without delay to Dublin, and place themselves under such protection as that prelate could afford. They took up their residence, for a short time, in Fisher's-lane, at the north side of the river. Thence they removed to Channel-row, in the same neighbourhood, to a house which had been formerly occupied by Benedictine nuns. Notwithstanding the dangers to which they were exposed, and the difficulties under which they laboured, they continued to increase in numbers. They devoted themselves to the education of young girls, as far as their opportunities allowed. Several elderly ladies, also, who wished to enjoy the consolations of religion in their declining years, placed themselves under their direction, and were boarded and lodged in an adjoining house, which formed part of the convent. In the year 1756, there were twenty-eight members in the community, besides pupils and boarders, and was presided over by Mother Elizabeth De Burgho, as prioress.

This community removed subsequently to Cabra. About thirty years since, it received permission from the Holy See to place itself under the jurisdiction of the Archbishop. At the present time it has reached a very high degree of efficiency and usefulness. Besides pupils who board in the convent, it has large schools for the education of the children of the poor. What is more meritorious, and of greater interest to the public, is their large establishment for the training of the deaf and dumb. Such an institution for the children of Catholic parents was long desired. The spirit of bigotry and intolerence infused into the minds of the pupils who were educated in the Protestant school of Claremont, was enough to shock every Catholic heart, and to outrage every Catholic feeling. It was felt that an effort should be made to correct this state of things, and rescue the poor Catholic deaf mute from the alternative that awaited him of ignorance on the one hand, or perversion upon the other. That effort was made, and succeeded. The Deaf and Dumb School of Cabra is its result, and is a glorious monument of the zeal and intelligence which led to its erection.

The ocnvent of Cabra has sent forth, as filiations, the communities of Kingstown, Booterstown, and Usher's-quay, Dublin, who devote themselves to the education of young ladies, and have large and flourishing schools.

After sending some of their body to Dublin in the beginning of the last century, as has been just mentioned, the rest of the Galway community remained for several years exposed to great privations and without any fixed abode. Their venerable prioress, Joanna Nolan, had been taken from them in the year 1701, at the advanced age of ninety, and was succeeded in her charge by the beloved companion of her toils, Mother Mary Lynch. By frequent change of residence, they succeeded in baffling the persevering pursuit of their enemies, and, by the holy and blameless tenour of their lives, they won, in course of time, the good opinion of those who, at one period, were their bitterest persecutors. The progress of time also allayed many of the angry elements of religious and political strife that convulsed

the country. Perhaps we may say, also, that men began to
grow ashamed of hunting to the death a body of poor harmless
ladies, some of them connected with the noblest families in the
land, and who wished for nothing but to be allowed to serve
God in peace and tranquillity. But this we know, that after
some years subsequent to their dispersion, the scattered members
of the flock formed themselves again into a body in Galway;
that they resumed once more their religious exercises; that they
were joined by other ladies who aspired to religious perfection;
that, despite all the perils of their position, and through all the
vicissitudes of their country, they maintained their conventual
existence unbroken; and that, after more than a century and
a-half of difficulty and privation, the Dominican nunnery of
Galway is now in a firm and flourishing condition.

When the convent of Galway was broken up, as we have
seen, in the year 1797, it reckoned among its members Sister
Catherine Plunkett. This lady, instead of taking shelter in the
home of her relatives, like many of her companions, repaired to
a convent of her order, near Brussels.   There she remained until
the year 1722, when the superioress of the Dominicans, wishing
to restore an old foundation in the town of Drogheda, directed
her to proceed to that place, and establish there a branch of her
institute.   She obeyed, and was soon joined by others who, by
their zeal and piety, raised the young establishment to a high
degree of celebrity. The distinguished foundress died on the
1st July, 1757, but before her death she had the satisfaction of
seeing her convent increasing in fame and usefulness, frequented
by numbers of young pupils, anxious to receive within its
walls a solid and Christian education, according to the standard
of the time, and increased by many fervent novices, who promised to perpetuate the works of religion and charity, when she
would be taken away from amongst them.   Thus it has gone
on and prospered, and grown up into the large and respectable
community which it presents in our days.   Among the treasures

which it possesses, is one that will be ever precious in the estimation of every Irish Catholic—the head of the celebrated Archbishop Plunkett, who was executed at Tyburn, in the year 1681. It is preserved in a silver reliquary, and is occasionally exhibited to gratify the respectful curiosity of the tourist, or the reverential piety of the Catholic, in whose eyes the venerable prelate is not only a victim of the foulest injustice, but a martyr almost sainted of the religion to which he belongs.

POOR CLARES.

THE order of Poor Clares, or speaking more correctly, the second order of Saint Francis, was founded by that saint at Assisium, a town of Umbria, in the year 1212. Saint Clare, who was appointed first abbess, and from whom it derives its name, was, as is well known, a model of the strictest poverty as well as of the most rigid ascetical observance. In the course of a few years after her death, it spread over a considerable part of Europe, though when they were introduced into Ireland is not exactly known. There is mention made of one convent of the order as existing near Carrick-on-Suir previous to the general confiscation of monasteries in the sixteenth century. But others may have existed at the same time, though no mention be found of them in the public records; for, as it was a fundamental principle of their institute to possess no real property, their existence could be but slightly affected by that measure. It is probable that the mere house which formed their poor dwelling, was the only possession of. which they could be deprived, and that they had nothing else to tempt the rapacity of the Government.

It is certain, however, that about the year 1625, a small
colony of Clares, from the convent of Gravelines, established a
mission in Dublin. It consisted of but six members, and it
may be easily conceived that amid the religious and political
troubles of the time, their undertaking was attended with many
dangers and difficulties. Their convent, if the dwelling they
occupied be entitled to that designation, was located in Ship-
street, in that city. Two years after their arrival, they were
compelled to leave the metropolis, and seek shelter and security
in the solitude of the country. Fortunately for them, one of
the professed sisters was a near relative of Sir Luke Dillon,
and he, in consequence, afforded them the charity of his
protection. He also assisted them in building a small convent,
near the town of Athlone. To this humble and unpretending
erection they gave the name of Bethlehem, hoping probably
that it would become the cradle of a better order of things for
religion and themselves. Being in the midst of a Catholic
population, their number soon increased, and in a very few years
the community consisted of sixty-one members. In the year
1633, they established a house in Drogheda, and in 1641 they
sent a colony to Galway. When they were thus establishing
themselves in fancied security, they little thought that a storm,
such as had not yet been seen, was about to burst over the Irish
Church, and that a new Herod was about to lay his rude hand
on their dear Bethlehem, to carry terror and desolation into its
borders. Beneath the iron rule of Cromwell, these young
communities were completely scattered to the winds. Some of
the nuns went back again to their own families, others were
driven to the shores of Spain and Belgium, where multitudes of
the clergy and of the religious orders of both sexes, were
received with welcome. When the second Charles was restored
to his throne, and that peace seemed likely to follow the new order
of government, the surviving members of the Poor Clares, in
common with many others, sought to gain possession of the
homes from which they had been so rudely and unjustly expelled.

They were successful in Galway, but it was only to a very limited extent, and their tenure long continued to be disturbed by alarms for their personal safety, as well as by a general insecurity of possession. The convent of Galway, however, exists to the present time, and is looked on as the parent house of the other Clares in Ireland.

In the year 1712, it was deemed advisable to transfer part of the community from Galway to Dublin, with the hope of being more free from vexatious annoyances in the large and populous city, than they were likely to be in a provincial town, where they would always be under the eyes of the municipal authorities. In this they were doomed to disappointment. They had to remove more than once from house to house, to escape the domiciliary visits of the authorities and the impertinent intrusion of unauthorized individuals, who wished either to gratify their bigotry, or to gain favour with the Government by an affected display of zeal. These vexatious annoyances they continued to be exposed to, and had occasionally to endure down nearly to the beginning of the present century. In 1803, they removed to their present convent at Harold's-cross, where their long career of social and political troubles has found at length a happy and, it is hoped, a final termination. In the year 1830, they established a branch at Newry, which house is worthy of note in one respect, namely, that it is the first convent founded in the north of Ireland since the period of what is popularly called the Reformation, and measures have been taken for establishing a new foundation in the town of Cavan, which have already been attended with success.

When the Clares were transferred to Harold's-cross, the Most Reverend Dr. Troy, then Archbishop of Dublin, was very desirous to enlist their services in the education of the Catholic poor. He accordingly solicited and obtained from the Holy See a brief, bearing date the 10th of June, 1804, exempting them from the obligation of reciting the divine office of the Church, to which they were until then bound, and directing

them to say in its stead the little office of the Blessed Virgin
Mary. By it they were also dispensed from many fasts and
austerities of their rule, which were commuted into the equally
laborious and more practically useful obligation of works of
charity to the poor. They have accordingly a large orphanage,
where a hundred poor children are brought up in the knowledge
and love of God, and formed betimes to the regular and pious
fulfilment of Christian duty. They have also attached to
their several convents large and well-attended schools, in which
they devote themselves with much success to the religious and
moral education of the poor.

The Clares were founded by Saint Francis, for the especial
practice of religious poverty. This was to be the peculiar feature
by which they were to be distinguished from all other conventual bodies. They were to be known through future ages
as the order of Poor Clares, and to be, as their name indicated,
poor in the truest and most perfect spirit of the Gospel. They
were to spend their lives in the practice of heavenly contemplation, and of all the rigorous austerities of true poverty, as well
as of religious asceticism. To attain this spirit more thoroughly,
as well as to secure its perfect observance against all temptations
to indulgence, they were bound to refrain from all conventual
property, and to depend solely for subsistence on the alms of
the faithful. This they continued to do for several centuries,
and they still adhere to it in those countries where such an observance is possible; but, in a state of society like ours, and in
such uncertainty and danger as they have been exposed to
in our land, it is evident that a mode of subsistence so precarious
would soon end in their ruin and dispersion. This rule has,
therefore, been prudently relaxed; and in Ireland, and probably
also in several other countries, they are permitted to have as
much property as will secure to them the necessaries of life, and
enable them to devote themselves to their works of charity without having the chance of starvation staring them in the face; but
they are, notwithstanding, still strictly bound to the true and

perfect religious poverty which forms the distinctive character of their institute.

A convent of Poor Clares has lately been established in Kenmare, which is presided over by Mrs. O'Hagan, and has done much good to the poor of the town.

CARMELITES.

WE are informed by the learned and laborious Alban Butler, in his Lives of the Saints, that there were no convents of Carmelite nuns in existence until the year 1452. About that time the Venerable John Soreth, a Carmelite of great zeal and sanctity, formed several establishments for such females as wished to follow his rule. One of these was at Liege, in the present kingdom of Belgium, and another at Vannes, in Brittany. These nuns soon extended themselves into many other provinces of the Christian world. But, in course of time, the fervour of their primitive discipline having become much relaxed, the celebrated Saint Teresa undertook the work of reform, and effected it, as is well known, with a most wonderful success. Since her time, and in consequence of her reform, the order has become separated into two great divisions: one called the Barefooted Carmelites, who follow her rule; the other called the Grand Carmelites, who continue to adhere to that which had been previously observed. Each of these has also become divided into other branches, which adhere more or less strictly to the letter of their rule, while all seek to preserve its original spirit, as adapted to present times and circumstances. Some, like the convent of Ranelagh, for instance, observing strict seclusion, avoiding all intercourse with seculars, except on most necessary occasions, and even then with all the precautions of the most exact cloister life, and devoting themselves almost without interruption to the exercises of prayer and meditation. Others, following a much more mitigated observance, and scarcely differing in any important particular from those other orders who devote them-selves to education. Some again are subject to the jurisdiction of the friars of their order, according to their ancient institute, while others have been placed under the episcopal jurisdiction of the diocese in which they are situated, and acknowledge no ecclesiastical authority but that of the ordinary and the Holy See.

There are authentic monuments in existence which prove that the Carmelite nuns had a convent of some kind in Dublin as early as the year 1661; but it is now impossible to ascertain whether they came to Ireland before that period, and under what circumstances they were first introduced. It is certain, however, that their condition must have been, like that of all the other religious bodies then existing in the country, a very dangerous and troubled one, and that they depended for subsistence on such precarious resources as the labour of their own hands or the bounty of their friends afforded. The works of charity which they would wish to perform they could only do in secret, so that even their left hand was not to know in what their right was employed. Where the sphere of their usefulness was so limited and so beset with perils, it was not to be expected that they should exercise any very extensive or important in-fluence on the religious condition of the people. It was much to maintain their ground and provide for the continuance of their institute.

· But, as the restrictions of the penal laws were diminished, the Carmelites began to share in the blessings of freedom that began thereby to be enjoyed by all. They opened schools for the education of the people. They began to enjoy increased facili-ties for the exercise of their religion. They gradually emerged from the obscure lanes, where alone they were able to enjoy security, into the healthier localities of the neighbouring country. They were joined, without fear of molestation, by such ladies as wished to devote themselves to the service of God and His poor, and became, in due course of time, what we now find them— useful, edifying, and prosperous institutions; centres of charity and religion in the several localities in which they have been established. The Carmelite nunneries of Ireland are eight in number, seven of which in the immediate vicinity of Dublin, and the other in the town of Loughrea, are all engaged in the great work of education.

URSULINES.

THE Ursulines date their origin, not from Saint Ursula, whose name they bear, but from Saint Angela of Merici, or, as she is sometimes called, Angela of Brescia, from the town of that name in the north of Italy, where she first commenced her labours. She was born in the village of Dezenzano, within six leagues of Brescia, and in the diocese of Verona. She devoted her life to the instruction of the young, from a sense of its urgent necessity in the actual circumstances of her country. She formed her associates into a kind of religious sisterhood, which was to devote itself to the education of the poor, and to such other works of mercy as their spiritual and corporal wants required. Shortly after her death, which happened in 1540, the institute was approved of and confirmed by Pope Paul III., a short time after he had approved the Society of Saint Ignatius of Loyola. He formed it into a religious congregation, under the name of Saint Ursula.

By the early constitution of this body, it scarcely differed from what is now designated a confraternity or association of pious females. Their duties were to be, to visit the sick and indigent in their own homes; to exhort sinners, especially of their own sex, to repentance, and to instruct the young. For the latter purpose they established schools, which were frequented by the rich as well as the poor. Each member of the pious sisterhood had her own work of charity assigned to her, and on Sundays they all met in some convenient oratory or chapel for their religious exercises. Here, also, they gave a report of their proceedings during the week that was just expired, and received their instructions for that which was to come. They had no common residence, and each member lived on her own means, and in the home of her relatives or friends. They did not even assume any distinctive form of dress until nearly two years after the confirmation of their institute by Paul III.

The illustrious Bishop of Milan, Charles Borromeo, at once saw their value; and in the year 1568, succeeded in procuring a sufficient number to found an establishment in his diocese. He formed them into a regular community, wearing a similar dress, living under the same roof, and practising together the usual exercises of a religious life. In Milan their labours were principally directed to the duty of education; and their improved system and unremitting attention soon won for them the most distinguished success, and were the theme of universal admiration. In 1572, he procured from Pope Gregory XIII. a brief confirming the arrangements he had made for their conventual existence, and enjoining the conventual enclosure, then recently and strongly commanded by the Council of Trent to all communities of religious women.

These regulations were, however, not of long continuance. In the year 1576, the great plague visited the city of Milan, and the important duty of charity to the sick and dying took precedence of every arrangement of mere religious discipline. The Ursulines—for they were so called by their foundress—were summoned by their holy bishop to the aid of the sick and dying, and were inferior to none in the heroic self-sacrifice and devotion which marked the conduct of the clergy and the religious bodies during that terrible visitation. During those dreadful days, when death was in every house, and hundreds were swept away to the grave in one common promiscuous mass, without distinction of age, or sex, or rank, or condition, the Ursulines were to be seen everywhere employed in those acts of charity demanded by the occasion. When the plague passed away, the example of heroic virtue which they afforded, recommended them so strongly to the favourable notice of the public, that branches of their order were introduced into many of the other cities of Italy, and some even into the south of France. The convent of the Rue St. Jacques, in Paris, was the principal house of the order in the latter kingdom, and was founded early in the seventeenth century. It followed exactly the rule given by St. Charles to the convent of Milan, and was the parent house of most of the communities of Ursuline nuns in France. It had been sixty years in existence, when an application was made to it by the Abbé Moylan, for a new foundation in Ireland. This application was made on behalf of Miss Nano Nagle.

Miss Nagle was born in the year 1728, at Ballygriffin, in the county of Cork. It was the family seat of her ancestors, and is beautifully situated on the picturesque banks of the river Blackwater. The family of that name, and of which Miss Nagle was one of the most honoured members, is well known in the south of Ireland. In the worst of times it was faithful to its religion, and is still in the enjoyment of much of its ancient inheritance. When so many of Irish blood have fallen away, it is no slight honour to have clung, through good report and through evil, to the venerable faith of its country. Her father was Mr. Garrett Nagle, of that place; and in the maternal line she is connected, through the Mathews of Thomastown, with the Reverend Theobald Mathew, the Apostle of Temperance in Ireland. Her parents were sincere and practical Catholics. The persecution they suffered from bad government, but attached them to their faith the more; and they took care to inculcate its principles on the tender and yet susceptible minds of their children. While still a child she gave some indications of a wayward and thought-

less levity, that more than once was a source of some concern
and uneasiness to her mother, but of which (if indeed it was ever
more than the ordinary waywardness of childhood) no trace can
be discovered in her maturer years, so completely had religion
softened, if not changed, the natural vivacity of her temper.
To her kind and indulgent, and probably more discerning
father, however, she was always an object of the most affectionate regard, for he did not expect to find the gravity of a woman
in one who was but a child. With the confidence of a parent's
heart he would often say, that his " poor Nano would be a saint
yet." This, which was nothing more than the outpouring of a
father's love, has derived from its subsequent fulfilment the character of a prophecy. When she received the scanty measure
of instruction which the domestic tuition of the times afforded,
and which probably went no farther than the mere rudiments of
knowledge, it was determined to send her to some one of the
Continental cities, to complete her education. Such a course was
then usual among persons of her class, who had no other means
of acquiring the useful and elegant accomplishments, which the
unhappy condition of the country rendered impracticable at
home. She was accordingly sent to Paris, then, as well as now,
the centre of the fashionable world, and to which, at that time
especially, the brilliant court of Louis XV. imparted a more than
ordinary splendour. The recommendation of influential friends
gained her admittance to some of the most select society of that
fascinating capital. The conduct of the Irish Government of the
day, very calamitously for itself, drove many of the best and
noblest families of the country into exile. Their exclusion from
any office of trust or emolument, the refusal of their civil and
religious rights, the open injuries and indignities to which they
were subjected after the perfidious violation of the treaty of
Limerick, made their residence in Ireland one not only of dis-
comfort, but of danger. If the sword of an Irish Catholic was to
win its way to wealth and fame, it was to be in other lands and in
another cause than the welfare or defence of his native country.

The history of many a well-fought field and arduous campaign, contain few names more illustrious than those which England drove with scorn and ignominy from her shores. Many of the Irish refugees or their descendants then adorned the French metropolis, and the Irish Society of Paris was numerous and fashionable. Miss Nagle devoted herself, with the unreflecting gaiety of youth, to its pleasures and its amusements. After some time, and when the more important purposes of her visit to the metropolis were effected, she seems to have largely shared in the customary round of visits, parties, and evening amusements. The delightful contrast which these afforded to the monotony of her own quiet country home, by the banks of the Blackwater—the charms of music and conversation, which Parisian life presented to the votary of pleasure—the attractions, ever-varying and ever-new, which a great city furnishes to one accustomed only to a simple rural life, made her present residence fascinating in no ordinary degree; and she suffered herself to be borne along the stream of enjoyment, absorbed in the present, and thoughtless of the future. She remained thus for some considerable time, and was at length rescued from the danger of her condition by an event trifling in itself, but important in its consequences to her, as well as to thousands then unborn. She had been spending the evening at a fashionable party; the entertainment was prolonged to a late hour; and when the company separated, she was wending her way homeward, in all the languor of weariness and exhaustion. The morning was still in its earliest dawn. The busy world was not awake, and the silence of the lonely and deserted streets was broken only by the roll of the distant carriage, that bore homeward some gay votary of fashion. Her way was through one of those narrow streets, which, even at the present time, intersect the city in every direction; and, on turning a corner, her attention was attracted by some poor people standing near the door of a church. They were a-foot thus early, to hear Mass before their day's work commenced. They were too early even for the porter who was

wont to attend their matin call; and they collected round the door
of the church, awaiting the moment of admittance.   Such a scene
is by no means new in Catholic countries, but at that moment it
was new and startling to her, and conveyed a serious and impressive lesson to her mind.   What a contrast, she thought, there
was between their simple, earnest, self-denying devotion, and
her frivolous, dissipated, she fancied criminal, course of life!
How differently they appeared in merit to that all-seeing eye,
that from the high arch of heaven looked down in ceaseless
watch on all!   How different would be their several destinies
hereafter!   How many hours did she pass away unprofitably,
that might indeed be converted to good use!   The thoughts
that crowded upon her soul were bitter and humiliating, but
they were salutary.   Her bosom heaved with emotion, and big
tears of regret began to flow down her young cheek.   In an
instant her heart was changed, and she determined on an entire
change of life, and resolved to devote herself for the future to
the service of God.

   This resolution of devoting herself unreservedly to God's service,
she never either regretted or altered.   As a natural consequence
of it, she withdrew herself from all the worldly amusements
and social festivities that had until then proved so fascinating,
and returned to her own country after a short interval.   Having
but few of the engagements of worldly life to occupy her time
and claim her attention, she employed herself in such works of
charity as her position enabled her to perform, and particularly
in the instruction of the poor.   It was during her stay at the
house of a friend, that the necessity for such instruction forced
itself on her notice.   She never could have believed, if she
had not seen it with her own eyes, and heard it with her own
ears, that the ignorance of the poor was as great as it really was.
The little knowledge they had of God and of religion, was obscured by many erroneous notions; and these brought, as usual,
in their train, many useless observances.   Miss Nagle was prepared to find ignorance among them, and disposed to make

every reasonable allowance for the effect of that political system
by which they had for centuries been, to use the expression of
an old writer, " brayed as it were in a mortar," yet she was
shocked at the scenes of moral and religious desolation that lay
before her Zealous individual exertion may, in some instances,
mitigate the evil, but its full remedy was far beyond any private
effort. The work in which she was then engaged, and the evident
necessity of making some lasting provision for the education of the
poor, first suggested to her mind the value of a religious community for that purpose; but it was then a mere passing thought,
which seemed far beyond her power ever to accomplish.

About the year 1750, which was the time now spoken of, the
people were sunk in the lowest state of political degradation;
the beginning of that century was, perhaps, the darkest period
in the history of the Catholics of Ireland.   They were silent,
indeed, and history makes no mention of their sufferings, but
theirs was the silence of despair. Their valour in the field
had been rendered ineffectual by the pusillanimity of their
leaders, or by internal dissension, the demon that had ever
blighted the destiny of Ireland. The rights reserved to them
by treaties and solemn covenants, were trampled on with scorn.
Even the corrupt and bigoted Parliament was quiet, not through
any good-will to the Catholics, but because its worst was done.
From the beginning of the religious dissensions, it had been the
policy of the Irish Government, aided by an obsequious Parliament, to discourage knowledge under the severest penalties.
By the laws then on the Statute Book of Ireland, and as far as
they could be rigidly enforced by the bigots in power, any one,
whether parent, tutor, or guardian, who should send a child for
education to any foreign seminary or private family, as also the
child so sent and educated, as well as the persons who would be
accessory thereto, were to be for ever disabled to sue or prosecute
in a court of justice in any action, civil or criminal, or to be
guardian, executor, or administrator; they were to be incapable
of making or receiving any legacy, deed, or gift; and, moreover,

to forfeit all property, both real and personal, during the term of their natural lives. The education of a Catholic was, in the eye of the law of Ireland, a crime of such enormous magnitude, as to require, as the only fitting penalty, a total forfeiture of the rights of citizenship; and the person so guilty was to become an utter alien to all the privileges of civil society. Was it to be wondered at that a people, subject for years to laws like these, should be reduced to the state in which Miss Nagle found them on her return from the Continent?* The religion which could have remedied, or at least mitigated, the evil, was even more rigorously proscribed. The same laws which made education a felony, denounced the pastor and set a price upon his head; and the few lessons that could be given were to be only by stealth, as if they were some bad and wicked thing, and at hurried and distant intervals, such was the fearful insecurity of the times. They were like the seed sown among thorns and brambles, choked up and unattended to, and consequently bore no lasting fruit. The want of popular and religious instruction was, therefore, great and pressing; but how difficult was it to be supplied? Any attempt on the part of Miss Nagle, with little chance of being successful, would have drawn down upon her the severity of the laws, and endangered the security, not only of herself, but of all connected with her; while her own position, which was one of dependence upon her friends, did not afford her the means necessary for the purpose. She would most cheerfully have given her personal services; but how far would these meet the magnitude and urgency of the want? Dismayed

---

* " Whilst this restraint upon foreign and domestic education was part of a horrible and impious system of servitude, the members were well fitted to the body. To render men patient under a deprivation of all the rights of human nature, everything which could give them a knowledge or feeling of those rights was rationally forbidden. To render humanity fit to be insulted, it was fit that it should be degraded. Indeed, I have ever thought the prohibition of the means of improving our rational nature, to be the worst species of tyranny that the insolence or perverseness of mankind ever dared to exercise. This goes to all men, in all situations, to whom education can be denied."— *Burke's Letter of an English Commoner to a Peer in Ireland.*

by the evils which surrounded her, and unwilling to be an eye-witness of the misery which it was not in her power to relieve, she determined on seeking, in the bosom of some religious community on the Continent, that opportunity of serving God in peace, which her own country could not afford her. Like the afflicted daughter of Sion, weeping by the river of Babylon, she could there mourn, in the silence of God's house, over the hapless lot and spiritual desolation of her people.

She took leave of her friends for ever, as she thought, and set sail for France. We do not know whether she had in view any one form of the religious life in preference to another; but were we to judge from the tenor of her acts, and the nature of her dispositions, it is probable that some religious order which was immediately connected with the poor, would have been selected by her, if the choice depended on herself alone. But Providence arranged it otherwise. Though she had accomplished one part of her object, by removing to France, she had yet some mis-givings as to its propriety. Her heart was still in Ireland; and her thoughts were constantly absorbed in reflections on the wants of its benighted children. It was a prayer for their welfare that started to her lips in the morning; and her evening examen was never performed without an act of compunction at their supposed desertion. A dim and shadowy consciousness of having culpably abandoned them to ignorance and crime, haunted her very dreams by night. Was this strong and vivid feeling a witnessing of the divine will in her regard, or was it, what on soberer reflection it seemed, but a mere spiritual delusion? What else could be the idea of doing what, in her circumstances, and with her means, seemed impossible? What could one lone woman, without talent, without assistance, with-out any great physical strength (for her health was far from good), accomplish for the improvement of her people, when kings and princes, the rulers and the legislature, and the crafty and unscrupulous policy of a mighty empire, were all arrayed in opposition to her? How many dread and stern realities were

there to resist its accomplishment, and to destroy almost the
possibility of success? This internal struggle continued to harrass
her for some time. In the anguish of her mind, she sought light
and aid from above, and advice from some experienced spiritual
guide. The members of the Society of Jesus were then, as
indeed they have always been, deservedly celebrated for their
learning and piety, and she had recourse to some of that body
in Paris, who had the reputation of being enlightened directors
of souls, to clear up her doubts, and disclose to her the path
of duty, in which God would have her walk. She consulted
more than one; and the objects of her choice proved themselves
in every respect worthy of the trust reposed in them. Perhaps
a special grace was vouchsafed to them upon an occasion
thus critical, where God's glory and a nation's spiritual good
depended so immediately upon their decision. The names are
not known of those to whom she laid open (the words are those
of one who knew her well) the agitation of her mind, her
settled disgust for the world, her ardent desire for the religious
state, her feeling for the poor of her own country, her strong
anxiety to contribute to their relief; so that, from the first
moment she discovered their ignorance, she could never divest
herself of the anxiety. But she attributed these ideas to her
own weak imagination; for, as matters then stood, it was morally
impossible for her to be of service to them. The penal restraints
were an insuperable bar, and she had no pecuniary resources of
her own. Her constitution, also, was delicate. To expose
herself again to the dangers of the world upon so poor a prospect
of success, was hazardous in the extreme; still she felt herself
most strongly impelled to it, nor could she turn her thoughts in
any other direction. When she had thus laid down all her load
of uneasiness, and explained the state of her mind, far from
being encouraged by them to embrace the religious state, they
unanimously declared that to instruct poor children in Ireland was
doubtless the object of her vocation; that her profound humility,
her solid judgment, the steadiness of her virtue, aided by divine

grace, would be ample protection against the dangers of the world; that though her fortune was not then extensive, her opulent connexions may one day augment it; that to co-operate with Christ in saving many souls, was certainly more glorious than to confine her efforts to the saving of her own; that so generous an example must have its share of influence, and that though the penal laws might prevent her from doing as much as she wished, they could not prevent her from doing what lay in her power. She argued—she remonstrated, but to no purpose; their decision was not to be changed. The issue appears to indicate that this advice and decision were immediately suggested by the Spirit of God. The time, perhaps, was come at length when the prayers of the saints for their suffering and deserted brethren, were to be heard. At this period, there were few religious houses on the Continent in which there was not to be found some one of Irish birth or extraction, to supplicate heaven in behalf of his or her afflicted people; and to beg for them some share of those blessings of which they had been so long and so wantonly deprived. Miss Nagle was the instrument selected by God to accomplish His own wise ends. She was no sooner persuaded that her vocation was to minister to the wants of her own poor, than she came back to Ireland, and commenced that career of usefulness and piety which was never interrupted until her death. Not even her most sanguine anticipations could have conjectured the magnitude and importance of the good that was to result from her labours.

In the year 1745, a terrible calamity occurred in Dublin, which led to some slight mitigation of the penal laws against the Catholics. The public celebration of divine worship being prohibited, a number of people had assembled in a store in Cookstreet, to hear Mass on Patrick's day. The assembled crowd was so great, that the beams which supported the floor gave way, and the entire congregation were precipitated to the ground. Nine persons, including the priest, were crushed to death. Lord Chesterfield was the Viceroy at the time, and the sensation caused by this calamity, combined with his own sense of liberality, induced him to tolerate the opening of the Catholic chapels for the performance of divine service. It was an act of pity, not of justice, on the part of the Government of the day. The Incorporated Society, and similar bodies, had been established for the avowed purpose of bringing the poorer classes over to the Protestant religion. The Charter Schools were in active operation, on which enormous sums of money were bestowed by the State, and they had all the support and patronage that the maternal solicitude of the Established Church could give them. So great was the influence of the established clergy, that they would not permit any opposition, and the Government discountenanced, and the laws absolutely prohibited, any education by members of the Catholic persuasion. The natural and inevitable consequence of such a system, was the ignorance and degradation of the people; a degradation that would have been general and perpetual, but for the leaven of religion which still, despite the efforts of misrule, continued to pervade and vivify the mass of the population. The following extracts from a somewhat rare work (the *Cork Remembrancer*), give some glimpses of the state of society in the South of Ireland, about the period when Miss Nagle commenced her schools. They prove the crying necessity there existed at the time for some effort to arrest the barbarism to which bad legislation was fast urging those who had the misfortune to be subjected to it. They are taken from a diary written at the time:—

" May 23, 1768.—Rioting had become so common, and arrived to such a height in this city, that it was supposed, if proper steps were not speedily taken, it would be unsafe for the inhabitants to walk in the streets, as the lawless vagabonds who engaged in such riots were most abandoned wretches, who scrupled not to commit any villainy. A number of these gentry assembled in a most riotous manner in Shandon churchyard this morning, but were dispersed upon one of them being shot dead, whether by one of the rioters, or by one of the annoyed inhabitants, is uncertain. There were likewise rioting and unlawful assemblies in other parts of the city, on this and the following day, in which several of the rioters were wounded, and innocent persons abused."

"Nov. 28, 1768.—For some weeks past a great number of idle vagabonds had annoyed the city by assembling in various parts of the suburbs on the Sabbath day, for the purpose of cutting and hacking, not only one another, but any of the inhabitants that may fall in their way."

"Dec. 3, 1769.—Rioting had become so common in this city, that it was not safe for any one to stand at his door without a weapon of defence."

"January 11, 1772.—A number of men this morning, with their faces blackened, and armed with hangers, bludgeons, &c., entered the shop of a respectable citizen near North Bridge, where they put out the candles, broke the shop windows, cut, spoiled, and carried off great quantities of his goods."

"March 7, 1772.—A man was killed in an affray this night, at the upper part of Mallow-lane."

"March 8, 1772.—One of the sentinels at South Gate was knocked down by three desperadoes, who (were it not for the noise of passengers approaching) would have thrown him over the bridge. The evening of the same day (to use the words of the newspaper) was concluded in a most pious and devout manner, by the warlike sons and daughters of Fair-lane and Blackpool, who met in a long field near Fair-hill, and fought with one another till night came on. The females were armed plentifully with stones; and the male inhabitants, according to Cherokee custom, with tomahawks of a new construction, which were about four feet long, and so dexterously contrived (having a hook and spear at the end) that any who missed grappling, were sure to stab with the sharp point."

"April 5, same year, the Fair-lane and Blarney-lane com-

E

batants met at Parkmore, according to *weekly* custom, and after
an engagement of some hours, one Reilly received a stab from
a tomahawk, by which he was instantly killed. Many on both
sides were wounded."

" May 1, same year, two men were killed in a riot between
the same people, who renewed the fight after the interment of
the deceased man. On the following day, they were going to
hang a Blackpool man, when he was rescued by the army."
(soldiers.)

These extracts will prove more convincingly than mere assertions, the state to which the people were then reduced, by the
demoralizing and barbarous policy of the Government, which
not only did not restrain these acts of violence, but would not
permit the application of a proper remedy. The very magis-
trates, who looked on with a passive indifference on such scenes
as these extracts describe, could even assemble a few years later
and deliberate on the necessity of extinguishing the germ of the
Ursuline and Presentation orders, which proposed to educate
the people. The tour of Doctor Young proves that it was no
better in the rural districts which he visited.

Miss Nagle had not been long at home, when she determined
on carrying into effect the object she had so much at heart. She
did so, however, in the strictest secrecy, and almost without the
knowledge of any of her family. After some time, one great
obstacle to her benevolent designs was removed, by the death
of her uncle, Joseph Nagle, who bequeathed to her a valuable
property. He was acquainted with her charitable dispositions;
and probably thought he could not apply it more usefully than
in placing it unreservedly at her disposal. The manner in which
her schools became known to the public and to her friends, is
very curious; and fortunately some of her own original letters
are in existence, in which it is described. The following is
an extract. The letter is dated the 17th of July, 1769,
and is addressed to one of the first members of the Ursuline

community. The remaining portions of it shall be given in their proper places:—

"Dear Miss Fitzsimons,—I am sorry Miss Coppinger cannot see the schools, as I think no one can have an idea of their use unless an eye-witness. As you wish to have a particular account of them, I will tell you how I began. I think I mentioned to you before that it was an undertaking I thought I should never have the happiness of accomplishing. Nothing would have made me come home but the decision of the clergymen, that I should run a great risk of salvation if I did not follow the inspiration. This made me accept of a very kind invitation of my sister-in-law to live with her. When I arrived, I kept my design a profound secret, as I knew if it were spoken of, I should meet with opposition on every side, particularly from my own immediate family, as to all appearance they would suffer from it. My confessor was the only person I told of it; and as I could not appear in the affair, I sent my maid to get a good mistress, and to take in thirty poor girls. When the little school was settled, I used to steal there in the morning. My brother thought I was at the chapel. This passed on very well, until one day a poor man came to him, to beg of him to speak to me to take his child into my school; on which he came in to his wife and me, laughing at the conceit of a man who was mad, and thought I was in the situation of a schoolmistress. Then I owned that I had set up a school; on which he fell into a violent passion, and said a vast deal on the bad consequences that may follow. His wife is very zealous, and so is he; but worldly interests blinded him at first. He was soon reconciled to it. He was not the person I most dreaded would be brought into trouble about it; it was my uncle Nagle, who is, I think, the most disliked by the Protestants of any Catholic in the kingdom. I expected a great deal from him. The best part of the fortune I have, I received from him. When he heard it he was not at all angry at it, and in a little time they were so good as to contribute largely to support it. And I took in children by degrees, not to make any noise about it in the beginning. In about nine months I had about two hundred children. When the Catholics saw what service it did, they begged that, for the convenience of the children, I would set up schools at the other end of the town from where I was, to be under my care and direction, and they promised to contribute to the support of them. With this request I readily complied; and the same number of children that I had were taken in, and at the death of my uncle I supported them all, at my own expense. I did not intend to take boys, but my sister-in-law made it a point, and said she would not permit any of my family to contribute to them unless I did so: on which I got a master, and took in only forty boys. They are in a house by themselves, and have no communication with the others. At present, however, I have two schools for boys, and five for girls. The former learn to read; and when they have the Douay catechism by heart, they learn to write and cypher. There are three schools where the girls learn to read; and when they have the catechism by heart, they learn to work. They all hear Mass every day, say their morning and night prayers, say their catechism in each school, by question and answer, all together. Every Saturday they all say the beads; the grown girls every evening. They go to confession every month, and to communion when their confessor thinks proper. The schools are opened at eight; at twelve the children go to dinner; at five they leave school. The workers do not begin their night prayers until six, after their beads. I prepare a set for first communion twice a-year, and I may truly say it is the only thing that gives me any trouble. In the first place, I think myself very incapable; and in the beginning, being obliged to speak for upwards of four hours, and my chest not being as strong as it had been, I spat blood, which I took care to conceal, for fear of being prevented from instructing the poor. It has not the least bad effect now. When I have done preparing them at

each end of the town, I feel myself like an idler that has nothing
to do, though I speak almost as much as when I prepared them
for their first communion. I find not the least difficulty in it.
I explain the catechism, as well as I can, in one school or other
every day; and if every one thought as little of labour as I do,
they would have little merit. I often think my schools will
never bring me to heaven, as I only take delight and pleasure in
them. You see it has pleased the Almighty to make me succeed,
when I had everything, as I may say, to fight against. I assure
you I did not expect a farthing from any mortal towards the
support of my schools; and I thought I should not have more
than fifty or sixty girls, until I got a fortune; nor did I think I
should have had a school in Cork. I began in a poor, humble
manner; and though it pleased the divine will to give me severe
trials in this foundation, yet it is to show that it is His work, and
has not been effected by human means. I can assure you my
schools are beginning to be of service to a great many parts of
the world. This is a place of great trade. They are heard of,
and my views are not for one object alone. If I could be of any
service in saving souls in any part of the globe, I would do all
in my power."

When this was written, she had been five years engaged in
the meritorious and useful labours to which she there refers.
Neither wet, cold, nor fatigue, could deter her from her work of
charity. She spent the day in her schools, superintending their
management; teaching, as she tells us, the young their catechism,
and the old, on many occasions, their prayers—even those
prayers which should be ordinary and familiar words in the
mouth of every Christian. Her visits were not unfrequently
prolonged to a late hour, after the schools were dismissed, in her
anxiety to impress the truths of religion on some hapless child
of poverty and misfortune. And on many a cold winter evening,
she was seen returning from her long protracted labours, at the
hour when the darkening twilight makes the slippery pathway

perilous to the benighted pedestrian. Her appearance on these
occasions, holding her lantern before her with one hand, and her
cloak around her with the other, was long remembered by the
residents of the localities in which her schools were situated.

Her health, so far from suffering, seemed to have improved
by her labours. The attack which at one period threatened the
most serious consequences, passed away without any bad result.
He who tempers the wind to the shorn lamb, gave her health
and strength to perform her self-appointed duties with perseverance, regularity, and efficiency. For some of the years that she was
thus occupied, she stayed with her own family, joining in their
social festivities, and enjoying, with a Christian gaiety, the society
of her friends. But she never omitted her customary duties, for
any object of relaxation. They were the primary objects of her
care; and were always fulfilled in the early part of the day. But
she soon resigned all participation of the pleasures of society, and
withdrew herself gradually from all those offices which mere
worldly etiquette requires. She paid no visits, except when
charity suggested them, or her neighbour's good or edification
required. Her time was divided between her own religious
duties, and the care of her poor children. She had no greater
delight than in speaking to them of God, or in expressing the
hopes and wishes of her heart to Him, whether in the privacy
of her chamber, or in the presence of the adorable sacrament of
the altar.

Yet the schools she founded were to be at best but temporary.
She may devote her time, her means, her whole individual
attention to the education of the poor; but she herself was the
sustaining principle of the entire system which she had been
instrumental in constructing; and if she were taken away, the
entire would fall to the ground. In a few years that event
would, in the ordinary course of nature, take place. She had no
security that it may not be in a day. It was, therefore, a matter
of the most serious and urgent importance, to consider whether
some stability might not be given to it—firmer and more lasting

than it could derive from the life of any one individual. To unite with herself some other pious ladies, animated with a kindred spirit, would, indeed, give greater extension to her usefulness; but the adequate attainment of the object she had in view, could be secured only by means of a religious community. If such were attained, it would be a guarantee both for its fullest efficiency, and its continuance for generations to come. But if the mere establishment of a school, for the purpose of imparting elementary knowledge, was dangerous to the parties concerned therein, how much more dangerous would be the establishment of a religious community devoted expressly to the purpose? The very existence of a priest or a religious in the land was a thing of sufferance, connived at rather than permitted. It was not more than twenty years since, a proclamation was issued by the executive Government in Dublin, offering a reward of £150 for the apprehension of a bishop, £50 for that of a priest; and as if this blood-money was not enough, the conviction of any one who afforded shelter or protection to a bishop, was to be rewarded with the sum of £200. It is true these barbarous enactments had been inoperative for some years. But there was no legal immunity. The ministers of religion held their freedom by a single thread. They knew not when the cry of blood might be raised against them; and at the very period in question, the Catholics of Ireland had the misfortune to see a respectable and, as is now admitted, guiltless minister of religion, Father Nicholas Sheehy, parish priest of Clogheen, in the county of Tipperary, hunted to death by the Orange ascendancy, and with the connivance of the wretched Government of the day. Her plan was a bold and arduous thing to attempt, much more to carry into effect. She communicated her wishes to those who in every trial and difficulty had been hitherto her guides. One of these was the Rev. Mr. Doran, a member of the Society of Jesus; the other was his nephew, the Abbé Moylan, afterwards Bishop of Cork. To these zealous and enlightened guides, she submitted the desires of her heart. They entered warmly into her views;

and after a full consideration of the objects to be accomplished
and the dangers to be encountered, the Rev. Mr. Doran suggested
that no institute would be more suited to their position and their
wants, than a community of Ursuline nuns.

Many and serious difficulties soon presented themselves to her
view. There was, in the first place, the unsettled state of the
kingdom, to which reference has been already made, and which
rendered the condition of a religious community one of imminent peril. Another difficulty more immediately affecting the
establishment, was that of procuring subjects for such a mission.
None of the professed religious of the convents to which application was made, would volunteer for so dangerous and laborious
an undertaking. When every other resource had failed, it
was arranged that some novices should be procured and received
into the house of St. Jacques. They were to be there trained
to the discipline of a convent life, and to the mode of conducting
schools. When this training was completed, it was hoped that
the foundation would not be attended with much difficulty.
The Abbé Moylan had the good fortune to meet with a few
generous and disinterested individuals, who were willing to run
every temporal risk, and encounter every temporal inconvenience, to forward the interests of religion. Their names deserve
a place in the history of their country. They were four in
number: Sister Angela Fitzsimons, Sister Augustine Coppinger, Sister Joseph Nagle, a relative of the foundress, and Sister
Ursula Kavanagh. They were all nearly connected with the
first families of the kingdom. Miss Kavanagh was very nearly
allied to the illustrious house of Ormonde. Miss Fitzsimons was
at that very time in Paris, for the express purpose of entering the
order of the Visitation, when Providence directed her attention to the religious wants of her own country and people. On
the 5th September, 1769, they all commenced their noviciate in
the convent of St. Jacques. The difficulties that beset the institution, may be inferred from the following letters of Miss
Nagle. The first is dated the 17th July, 1769, some months

before they entered on their noviciate, and is directed, as are indeed all the others, to her dear Miss Fitzsimons:—

" As it is always a real pleasure to me to hear from you, I am much obliged to you for both your kind favours. In the first, there was enclosed your note. I can't help saying that if I could be jealous at anything you did in my regard, it would be by your not writing in a more friendly manner; as, be assured, you may command anything in my power. I cannot express how much I suffered on your account, as I was sure your uneasiness must be great at not hearing of the arrival of the young ladies I mentioned. They were to depart in the first vessel that sailed to Havre. When I wrote I thought every thing was settled, but it has pleased God to order things otherwise, which, in all appearance, has turned out a fortunate occurrence; for by the delay there are two subjects more, such as one might ambition in every respect. I shall say nothing of their merit, as that will speak for itself. I am not acquainted with Miss Coppinger. I have seen her; but it is on the amiable character Mr. Doran gives her I depend: and I am afraid I shall not have the pleasure of seeing her again before she goes, as the measles are like a plague here. Though not always mortal, yet they are dangerous to grown persons; and Mrs. Coppinger told me it was the only disorder she dreaded for her daughter. She and the father are greatly pleased at her choice of life, they are so pious. I wished Mr. Shea was so well pleased at his daughter's inclination. He has not yet given his consent. He says it is a sudden thought. He does not know it long, though she has been thinking of becoming a religious more than twelve months. She is a person of incomparable sense and prudence, and it is not very probable she will change. Miss Coppinger's parents will not let her go, until her aunt Butler approves of her resolution, to which (by what you mention of her good intentions towards this foundation) she will immediately give her consent. . . . Had I only a proper person to begin this foundation, I think it has the prospect of meeting with surprising success. I am charmed with the account you give me of the ladies you are with. I hope the same spirit will be communicated here. I think religious discipline would be too strict for this country; and I own I should not rejoice to see it kept up. I must say Miss Moylan's prejudice to take on here, has made me see things in a clearer light than I should have done; and makes me accept the disappointments I have met with as a decree of the divine bounty. All her friends are sorry she went abroad; and I must say, laying aside her own merit, this house would have a great loss in her, as she is of a family deservedly beloved. They are in hopes she is beginning to change. I wish it may be so. If she has so much zeal, she will never have such an opportunity of exerting it as here. I must look on it as one of my crosses, that the two ladies who were so good as to patronize this foundation should be removed; but the Almighty is all-sufficient, and will make up this loss to us. I beg you will present them my compliments. Mr. Moylan desires to be affectionately remembered to you. As he gave you an account of the building, I shall say nothing of it, only to excuse myself as to the house I built first. I never intended it for ladies. At the time, I was sure I should get the ground at the rere to build on, and as it gave on the street, I was obliged to have it in the manner it is, in order not to have it noticed as a convent. I shall refer you for that and many other things to my next, which I hope the young ladies will be the bearers of. And believe me your affectionate friend,

" NANO NAGLE."

This Miss Moylan was a sister of the Abbé, afterwards Bishop Moylan, and the very first who joined the young community when it arrived in Cork. She lived within the convent walls for the unusual period of seventy-two years; and for much of that time held the responsible office of mother superior of the sisterhood. She witnessed and shared its early struggles and difficulties, and lived to see its subsequent prosperity. She died, full of years and virtues, in the year 1842, in the ninetieth year of her age. The letter of which the young ladies were to be the bearers, has not been preserved; for the next we have, is dated the 13th May, 1770, some months after they had entered on their noviciate:—

" Dear Miss Fitzsimons,—I am glad to profit of any opportunity to assure you how pleasing it is to me, to acquaint you with anything I thought would be agreeable to you; as I am certain it will be to hear, that I hope we have got a very desirable subject in the young lady I mentioned to you some time ago, recommended by Mr. Austen. I wish I could transmit to you that part of his letter, in respect of her, that he wrote to Mr. Doran; but as it was not convenient to give it to me, I shall give you a full account of her, and some conjectures of my own in her regard. As you may be surprised I have not insisted on a better fortune, and do not know how matters stand, I have done nothing in it but with the approbation of our worthy friend and your uncle. Her father will give only £200 to the house. He is to pay £15 a-year interest on it. While she lives, he is to give her a pension for herself, that he does not choose to name at present. His indignation is so great against her for being a nun, that he offers her £2,000 if she will marry. Her inclination, I find, was to go to the same convent where she was brought up. He would not consent to it, as he says there is a probability that in France they may demolish all the monasteries. He consented that she should go to Flanders; and Liege was the place he chose for her. I suppose, being under an ecclesiastical prince, he thought they would longer subsist. All these objections made her determine I believe on taking on here, and she is greatly pleased to be among those that were educated in France. When he gave her leave to come here, he desired that she should leave Dublin in July, and go to a convent in Galway, to remain till things are fixed here,

I have begged that she would come here, and stay with me.
In the first place, she could be of great service, and it would
be a great comfort to me to have her. It is considered more advisable for many reasons, in consequence
of his odd manner of acting in her regard. The footing I put
it on is its being less expensive than her going to Galway and
coming thence here. If he thought it would be agreeable to
her, I dare say he would let her come. She is his only child, and
I believe the same person we mentioned to you about two years
ago. There is a great likelihood that she will be of vast service
to the house. Her name I do not know. She has had a mind
to be a nun since she was a child, and is very devout. Nobody
can write better than she does. This is what Mr. Austen says
of her in the last letter in which he spoke of her. He said she
had great talents. Providence has ordered everything for the
best in her regard, to keep her for this place. It mortified me that
she had not joined you; and had she, I am sure she would have
met with the same fate the others did. Even Mr. Austen heard
so much to the prejudice of this foundation, that I believe he
did not endeavour to prevail on her, as he would, had he known
how matters were. Ever since Mr. Halloran has been here,
who was informed of the truth of everything, nobody can
interest himself more than he does for its success. We must
think the Almighty permits everything for the best. You will
see, with His assistance, everything turn out well; and His divine
hand will uphold us in getting your former mistress. The
house she is in will, in my opinion, bring a judgment upon
itself, if it hinder her from being the means of saving so many
souls. Mr. Moylan desired me to assure you of his most affectionate compliments. He is so hurried since the Jubilee, that
he has scarcely time to eat his meals. He attempted several
times to try to get an hour to sit down and write to you. It
was in vain. It mortifies him he cannot; as I don't know any
one for whom he has a higher esteem. His health is much
impaired since this great fatigue. He expects his sister every

moment; and will have time to write to you, and to the superior at the same time, as the Jubilee will be soon over. I was surprised when he asked me if I wrote to the mistress of novices. I never did. I know I ought to have done so, and to the superior. My not writing French prevented me, as I am very unwilling to be troublesome to those who I know have not time to spare, and I could not trust any one else. I hope your fortitude will bring you through all crosses, and put a happy conclusion to this foundation. Be not discouraged from choosing any young lady you think proper. I have been often ashamed for fear you would have thought I was in any way flattering you with the success of it. I met so many disappointments; and even that very young lady I now mention, I was sorry that we ever spoke of her to you, though we were sure of her when we did, and afterwards she was resolved to go to France. You see we have got her back again. And if Miss Smith be not entered into any other convent, Mr. Moylan thinks he can prevail on her to come here. I sincerely wish he may. I beg you will be so good as to present my compliments to the superior, to your present mistress and to your former one, whom I love and reverence, and to Mr. Fitzsimons. My best wishes attend the young ladies. All the family at Barryscourt are in perfect health, and Miss Nagle's family are also well. I hope you and they enjoy, as I wish you may always, perfect good. It gives me a vast deal of trouble to find that these two young ladies, that want to learn, can have no advantage in that respect. If it would be permitted there to have any body to teach them anything you thought would be hereafter an advantage to the house, don't spare any expense. You'll be the best judge of that, and of everything else in their regard. They are happy to have a person of your good sense to direct them; and I can say with truth, that you are, under God, the chief support of this good work, which I flatter myself you will see prosper

F

far beyond what one has a right to expect in such a country as this.

"I am, my dear Miss Fitzsimons,

"Your most affectionate friend,

"NANO NAGLE."

It will be seen by the latter part of this letter, how solicitous she was about the literary as well as the religious training of those who were to found her new establishment. This is in accordance with the good sense and wisdom which are observable in all her actions. The efficiency of any establishment intended for educational purposes, depends so much on the qualifications of those by whom it is conducted, that it is of the first importance that they be perfectly skilled in all those branches of knowledge which they will have to communicate to those entrusted to their care.

The next letter is dated Cork, September 28, 1770, and the latter part of it is wanting. In fact, the remaining letters, except one, are more or less defective. As usual, it is addressed to her dear Miss Fitzsimons.

"I am sorry it was not in my power sooner to tell you how much I am obliged to you for not standing on ceremony with me, and being so good as to write to me so often of late, though I could not answer your kind favours as punctually as I wished to do. I believe you'll attribute my silence to the real cause, which is want of time. I can't express the joy I had to hear of Miss Kavanagh's resolution, and that she had joined you. It was what you ambitioned this long time past. If once we were fixed, the object in view is so great, that I dare say many would follow your and her example. I had little reason, when first I thought of this foundation, to expect the success it has already met with. I must say, every disappointment we have had, the Almighty has been pleased to make it turn out to our advantage, though my impatience made me very often not

submit to His divine will as I ought. I believe we are indebted
to your worthy friend for this young lady's determination to
come here. We are happy, I think, in having one of the sisters.
I am not surprised at what you mention to me in regard of Mr.
Kavanagh, for he and his lady, by some conjectures of their own,
were sure Miss Nano intended coming here. As for my part, I
could not say anything that gave the least notion that she was
so inclined, nor did I flatter myself, by what the clergyman then
told me of her, that she would; and I must do her brother and
sister justice, they did not seem at all angry with her for it. I
dare say she will be of great service to her by her prayers. I cannot tell you how eager Mr. Doran is for your coming over soon,
as he foresees they will every day be starting some new difficulties on account of the French lady, which is already the case,
and was made an objection when Miss B. got leave to come. He
wrote to his nephew* the many reasons that make it so necessary
to have this establishment begun as soon as possible, as he and I
are sure, by the character you give of this lady, that she is one
of those modern religious persons who think every incon-
veniency is such a cross that there is no bearing it. She that
makes such a sacrifice for the good of souls, will have fortitude
to make light, I hope, of not having everything settled as com-
fortably as it ought to be. One could not imagine, in a house
so lately built, that the walls could be so dry as they are, nor
can one judge of those till they are plastered; for when the
plaster dries immediately, its owing to the walls being so. Had
I not seen it had this effect upon it, I could not have believed
it. You will find it will be very habitable this winter, which I
did not think it would be. And when you are settled there, I
shall be to blame if I do not get every necessary that is thought
wanting, as there is nothing in my power I shan't endeavour
to do. I hope you will be so good as to excuse in the beginning
all, and consider we are in a country in which we can't do as

* Dr. Moylan.

we please. By degrees, with the assistance of God, we may do a great deal."

"Cork, December 17, 1770.

"DEAR MISS FITZSIMONS,—It is not to be expressed all the anxiety of mind I have gone through by your and our worthy friend's silence, as I did not get the letter you mention to have been sent by hand; nor did I know what to think, till I had received yours of the 27th of last month. It did not surprise me to find by it that nothing was yet fixed, as I was sure I should soon be made acquainted with how matters went, if there was good news. On the receipt of your letter, I spoke to Mr. Doran, who is so good as to write in my name to the superior, begging her interest, and that she would be so charitable as not to defer making her community give a categorical answer. As to that point, I think she can't well refuse the last request in conscience; as to the other, she may not have any scruple about it. Had I written myself, she might say that I could do it as well before as on this occasion; and others may take it ill that I did not pay them the compliment. Only Mr. Moylan has such patience and zeal, he would certainly have long ago given up the affair. He is resolved to leave no stone unturned to bring about this foundation. He says you and he will consider what is best to be done, for I dread they never will consent to lose so useful a subject. Its all in the power of the Almighty. We don't know what is best for us, and so ought to be resigned to the divine will. I think I have reason to take it unkind of you, to give me so many reasons for making use of the credit I gave you on Mr. Waters, as you may be sure nothing could give me more pleasure than that I could in any way oblige you; and I beg you'll not be uneasy if Mr. Fitzsimons can't pay me readily, for money is at present so scarce, and such a run on the bankers in this kingdom, that people can't get what is due to them. I shall acquaint you when its paid. When one is in a strange country, any disappointment is sensible. As for my part, I am often without money, yet, as everybody knows me, I don't mind it.

"It gives me vast pleasure to find that Miss Kavanagh is so well pleased with teaching in the poor school. It shows a particular call from the great God to take delight in it. I dread, though her health is better, that in winter it will be too cold for her; and it would be better she should take care of herself for the good of the poor here, where she can be of more service than there; and I beg you will endeavour to prevent her from going to them. . . . . The young lady in Dublin, her name is Lawless. When everything was settled, F. Austen told it to her father, who came to town, but she could not prevail on him to come with her. He made an excuse that he was old and sickly, and the weather too cold for him to venture. He gave her leave to come when she got company proper for her to travel with. She was with an uncle of her's in James'-street. He engages not to let her want anything during her life. We were sure you were coming over, in consequence of reports that certainly you were on your way, until Mr. Doran inquired into the truth. I could have wished that when you determined not to come this winter, I had been informed of it; not so much on my own account, as on hers. I could not have avoided putting myself to some expense, and at a time when I had many calls for money, and employed workmen in the short days, which makes work come out vastly dear; and only, as I mentioned to you, that I was resolved not to buy what could be had in a few hours, and at farthest in a few days, I should have put myself to very unnecessary expense, which I am determined not to do till you are landed. That is a day I long for. It is a vast pleasure to me to find that your mistress is so much changed in her behaviour, as I think there is no greater happiness in the world than to be in union. Whoever we live with we must expect to have something to suffer, as this world is not to be our paradise. As I find they will allow you to leave when you have a mind, I hope that you and my cousin will get a person to instruct you in what may be useful to teach hereafter, if you should think proper. Give my best respects to Mr. Moylan, to your former mistress, to the superior, and to your present mistress. My affectionate compliments to all the young ladies. To Mrs. Lynch, when you see her, I beg you will say that my best wishes shall always attend her, and that I shall never forget all her kindness to me, which I have a grateful sense of. And believe me to be, with the sincerest esteem, dear Miss Fitzsimons, your most affectionate friend,

" NANO NAGLE."

In the summer of 1770, Miss Nagle repaired to Bath, on a short visit to her friends, who were then permanently residing at that place. She appears to have adopted this resolution after much hesitation, and if we may judge from her own words, with very considerable reluctance. Nothing would have reconciled her to even a temporary absence from her schools and children, but the hope of promoting by her presence the new institute, and recommending it to the good wishes and assistance of her friends. The next letter is dated Bath, July 20, 1770:—

" DEAR MISS FITZSIMONS,—Though I did myself the pleasure of writing to you lately, yet I do so now again, as a letter I received from our worthy friend makes me acquainted with the sudden death of his sister-in-law. She was a most amiable person, and I am most sincerely sorry for her. He says he is resolved to leave Cork in about twelve days, if the ship be ready and the wind fair. I always admired his zeal, and this is a great instance of it, to leave his afflicted family and tender father, all whose trouble for the death of his eldest son this shock revives, for if anybody ever died of grief, his daughter-in-law has. Yet notwithstanding Mr. M.'s fortitude to leave his friends in this situation, if his father, who is old and sickly, should fall ill, it won't be in his power to depart as soon as he expected, nor can I imagine it possible he will let him go, as he can hardly leave

him out of his sight, in this his urgent affliction. You thought
I came here for my health. As you are so good as to interest
yourself in my regard, and I was afraid it might make you
uneasy, I beg to assure you that, thank God, I never was better,
and it was not to take the waters I came, nor have I tasted them.
I came to see my brothers; and, be assured, it was with much
ado I could prevail on myself to pay them this visit. I did not
acquaint you with this tour, as I wavered so much with myself,
that I may say till I was in the ship I was not sure of coming.
It was so much against my inclination to leave my children;
and only to serve the foundation I never should have prevailed
on myself. Our friend, I have reason to think, spoke with a
prophetic spirit by what has happened, for my own family
would never have the opinion they have at present, nor ever
interest themselves as they do for its success. You must have
been surprised when you heard they knew nothing of it. You
heard what was true. The young lady who told you was the
first, my sister Nagle says, who told herself; and though she did
so, she could hardly believe her. You don't forget that I wrote
to you, that when I began my schools, my own immediate family
knew nothing of it; so the same method I was resolved to take
now. As I was sure they would be the first to oppose me, I
never said one word to them till I saw things had such a prospect of succeeding, which I was sure I never could have persuaded them of, if they did not see it. It gives them all great
pleasure that I should be the means of promoting such a good
work, and my sisters-in-law are as eager to get good subjects for
it as we could be. I hope you will approve of my manner of
acting, as the less noise is made about affairs of this kind in
this country the better. Mr. K—g got a letter from Dr.
Butler, on which he came to speak to me about his sister, and
says, as we must be of such service to the kingdom, if we had the
Protestants' consent for the establishment, he would be better
pleased she was amongst us, as she could do more good there
than anywhere else. On which I told him, before my brother

and sister, that had I consulted my own family, I should not have had a school in Cork, which they said was true."

The remainder of this very interesting letter is wanting.

The difficulties she encountered in the establishment of the Ursulines, may be still farther inferred from the following frag-ment of a letter written by her about this time. The first part is wanting, so that we cannot give its date; but, judging from the contents, it may be ascribed to the beginning of 1770:—

. . . . "As I always reflect on myself how many faults I have. How happy she was to have such a pious turn so early in life, and to have let herself be directed by that great servant of God, your former mistress, of whom I long to know whether she will do that meritorious action of settling this foundation. Her zeal is great. I am sure if she does it, she may be compared to the grain of mustard-seed in the Gospel. Though our house is the least in the order, it has it in its power to do more good than any; and the good seed she will sow will spread if she be inspired to it. I am sending boys to the West Indies. Some charitable gentlemen put themselves to great expense for no other motive. These boys being well instructed, and the true religion decaying very much there, by reason of those that leave this country knowing nothing of their religion, made them lay this scheme, which I hope may have the desired effect. All my children are brought up to be fond of instructing, as I think it lies in the power of the poor to be of more service that way than the rich. These children promise me they will take great pains with the little blacks to instruct them. Next year I will have pictures for them to give the negroes that learn the catechism. I must beg you will be so good as to buy me some dozens of the common pictures of that sort for them. I forgot to speak to Miss N. to send them to me by the first opportunity. I am glad she is liked by the ladies where she is. Had they known all she suffered for this foundation as well as I do, it would make them pass over many imperfections they may see in her. I am confident her intention is good. I run no risk in giving directions about her to a person of your piety and sense, as you may be confident that had I known the fille St. Joseph was a Jansenist, I should never have sent her there. I hope you will act in regard to the young ladies as you think proper, and be sure I shall always approve of it. I must say I was desirous they should learn what was proper to teach young ladies hereafter, as there is such a general complaint, both in this kingdom and in England, that the children are only taught to say their prayers. As for spiritual matters, I am sure the nuns will take good care of that. I must beg the favour of you, to present my compliments to the superior, to your mistress, and to your former one. My best wishes attend them and the young ladies. Had I the happiness of being looking at you, I should imagine you were laughing at me, to think I fatigue myself in the least. I can assure you I never thought there was the least trouble in acting in regard of the schools. Do not be uneasy about my health. Nobody can enjoy better health than I do, thank God. I must say I suffered a great deal in mind, which, for a time, I thought would have hurt my constitution, but it did not in the least. I am afraid you will all be tired of me, I may live to be so old. That is what is most to be dreaded. I beg you will believe me, with the sincerest esteem, your most affectionate friend,

"NANO NAGLE."

The reverential love, or, it may be, the fortunate accident to which we owe these precious fragments, has not rescued any more of these valuable and interesting letters from oblivion. Other channels must be had recourse to, less authentic, indeed, than her own words, but yet sufficient to enable us to continue with sufficient confidence the unbroken thread of the narrative.

The death of his brother's wife, and the advanced age and increasing infirmities of his father, detained Dr. Moylan in

Cork until the spring of the year 1771. Early in that year
he repaired to Paris, for the purpose of transplanting the germ
of his new community. Miss Fitzsimons had entered St. Jacques
on the 19th November, 1767; Miss Coppinger and Miss Nagle
on the 5th September, 1769; and Miss Kavanagh on the 4th
September, 1770. The first of these ladies had received the
religious habit shortly after her admission; the others only on
the 10th February, 1771. They had all acquired, as far as time
and circumstances would permit, the necessary knowledge for
conducting schools, and been accustomed to the duties of a
religious life, but deferred their profession until they should be
established in their own convent in Ireland. The difficulties to
which allusion has been made by Miss Nagle in her letters,
again presented themselves to impede and embarrass the undertaking. A professed religious was necessary for the foundation,
and not one member of the house at Paris could be had for the
purpose. One or two who had resolution, and were disposed to
contribute their services, were, through some interference, prevented from coming. Whatever the cause may have been,
there was no professed nun to accompany the young colony to
Ireland, and the object of the good abbé's mission seemed utterly
and irretrievably hopeless. Had he been less persevering or
zealous, he would, perhaps, have abandoned it altogether; and as
a reward of his perseverance, God was his helper and protector
in the hour of need. He was recommended to apply to some
of the other religious establishments in the French provinces, in
which there were many nuns of Irish extraction, for that, perhaps, some of those would be disposed to forward an undertaking
so useful to their people. In conformity with this suggestion,
an application was made, among others, to the Ursuline convent
at Dieppe, in Normandy. There was in that house a lady of
Irish birth, Mrs. Margaret Kelly, who immediately volunteered
her services, and consented to establish the foundation which
they had all so much at heart, by accompanying the young
colony to its destination, and presiding over it for a few years,

until it should acquire firmness and stability. Hence it has happened, that while the Irish Ursulines consider themselves a filiation of St. Jacques, the French writers consider them a filiation of the convent of Dieppe.

Having been thus far successful, arrangements were made for their final departure. It was appointed that their mother superior should meet them at Havre. Their first day's journey from Paris, so imperfect was then the mode of travelling, terminated at St. Denis, and their resting-place was the convent of the Carmelite nuns, one of the inmates of which, at that time, was Madame Louisa, the saintly aunt of Louis XVI. There are few more interesting or edifying narratives in the records of Christian sanctity, than the life of Louisa, the Carmelite of St. Denis. Born to rank and station as high as the world can give, her praise was hymned by a thousand flattering tongues, and more than ten thousand swords would have leaped from their scabbards to avenge any insult to her name. But hers was a heart which even the pleasures of a court could not corrupt. Feelingly alive to the uncertainty of human happiness, she abandoned all for God. For some years she had been practising, beneath the gilded ceiling of the Tuileries, rigorous austerities, to qualify herself for the state of life to which she aspired; and after a long life of holiness, during which her humility and goodness of heart, and unalterable sweetness of disposition, made her each day more dear to her sisterhood, she died in time to escape the horrors of that revolution, which burst with such fearful violence over her Church and people, and especially her own immediate family. How salutary an influence must her conversation and example have exercised on the young novices during the two days that they enjoyed her company! Such was her high opinion of their institute, that she said she would be glad to be at the feet of an Ursuline in heaven. She more than once declared, that if the circumstances of her position permitted, she would at once accompany them to Ireland. Sister Angela Fitzsimons had a voice of exquisite sweetness; and during her stay at the

convent, she delighted the religious more than once with the
exercise of her vocal powers.   The venerable walls of the little
convent church of St. Denis had been seldom filled with such
melody, as when the young Irish novice sang the anthem of the
Virgin, in the still and solemn hour of evening.   They reached
Rouen on the feast of St. Mark the Evangelist, in time to share
in the religious solemnities, which, on that day, were customary
in the Catholic countries.   Here they were joined, according to
previous appointment, by Mrs. Kelly, from Dieppe, and after a
few days delay they set sail from Havre, accompanied by the
Abbé Moylan, and after a voyage, which in those days must be
considered favourable, they arrived in the Cove of Cork on the
morning of the 9th of May, which in that year was the morning
of Ascension Thursday.   In compliance with the pressing
request of their friends, Miss Coppinger and Miss Kavanagh
proceeded, for a few days, to Barryscourt, a distance of five or
six miles, where their friends resided.   The other two, with
Mrs. Kelly, proceeded to Cork, where they were received with
much joy by their anxious and expecting friend, Miss Nagle.
The place intended for their reception not being yet ready, they
took up their residence in a house in the immediate neighbourhood, which was afterwards used by the Ursulines for the reception of visitors, and which is still employed for that purpose by
the Presentation nuns.   Here they were soon joined by their
companions from Barryscourt; and the convent being at length
prepared for their reception, and the necessary documents drawn
up between the community and Miss Nagle, they entered on
possession the 18th of September, 1771.   On the 22nd Mass, was
celebrated for the first time, and the Blessed Sacrament solemnly
deposited in the chapel.   Mrs. Kelly was appointed mother
superior, with the necessary authority; and thus, after many
trials and difficulties, and amid much of fervent joy and thanksgiving, was commenced the establishment of the Ursuline order
in this kingdom.

In December they were joined by two new subjects, Miss Daly, and Miss Moylan, to the latter of whom reference has been already made. In the month of January, and on the Monday immediately following the Feast of the Holy Name of Jesus, they opened for the first time their schools. Hence it is, that this day has been always a day of peculiar religious observance to the pupils of the convent. Their first class consisted of twelve pupils, who were the first-fruits of that rich harvest which the institute has since produced. They were the forerunners of many who, in after years, were to come from the East and the West, and the North and the South, to find knowledge and Christian perfection. At the present day, when so many efficient establishments, both secular and religious, may be had recourse to for the education of youth, persons may be led to undervalue the importance of the boon which was thus placed within the reach of the Irish Catholics. But if they carry back their thoughts to the middle of the last century, and contemplate the deplorable condition of the Catholics of that time, they will form a more correct estimate of its value. At this period, there was not one educational establishment of any consequence, to which Catholic children could be sent with safety. Those who sought the precious gift of knowledge, had to run many a risk, and brave many a peril, before it could be obtained. It was surely a hard trial to a father and mother's heart to part from their children, to sever those ties which bind them so closely at the age when it is most necessary that education should begin. It must have been surely a painful thing to send them across more than one stormy sea, and at a time when there were no steamers to shorten space and time, but when a voyage from Ireland to France or Belgium was a work of toil, and not unfrequently of danger; and it must have been hard to send them so far off among strangers, where, if sickness came upon them, there would be no mother's eye to keep watch over their fitful slumbers, and where, if death came upon them, as it often did, while yet the fresh sheen of childhood lingered on the cheek, they must have been consigned to the grave ere the fond parent, who expected from day

to day the return of its accomplished child, could be aware of
the event. It must have been a painful duty, even to those
parents who could afford it, to send their children abroad for
education. But what must have been the feelings and the condition of those whose means or position in society did not enable
them to do so? How keenly must they have felt the degrading
policy and barbarous legislation, which left them no alternative
but ignorance or apostacy for the members of their family!
They must indeed have sighed and prayed for any merciful
ordering of Providence, which should place the blessings of a
religious education within their reach. It is those only who
thus had prayed and suffered, not others, their more fortunate
descendants, that could appreciate the blessings and advantages
of the Ursuline institute to Ireland.

Many competent judges think that education, and female education more especially, can be best effected by means of an
enlightened religious community. Education does not consist
in the cultivation of the mental faculties alone, nor in the acqui-
sition of bodily accomplishments, however brilliant in themselves,
or laboriously acquired, but it consists in the combined and
judicious training of both mind and body. The difference between education and instruction may be inferred from the different results of each. The result of instruction is knowledge.
The result of education is character. It is not sufficient that
woman should know her duties, but she must also love them and
be able to perform them. She must make those duties easy to
herself, and useful and agreeable to all around her. She must
acquire that modest, amiable, winning power, which will give
her dominion over her peculiar sphere of duty. For her kingdom is in her own family, her empire is over their hearts. It is
not by the peculiar brilliancy of her attainments that she can
gain, much less secure that empire; for the qualities that dazzle
are not those most likely to attract and fascinate. She must be
formed to habits of punctuality and diligence in her ordinary
every-day duties; of charity and kindly consideration in her

intercourse with society; of profitable employment of time in her own home; and of practical religious principle and observance in all her duties and at all times. She should invest her little family circle with a charm powerful enough to attract the partner of her affections from the haunts of vice and dissipation; and her heart should beat with joy, and her eye brighten with affection, as he returns to it each day after his professional duty. Should adversity darken his worldly prospects, there should be at least one heart to feel his misfortune as its own. If God blesses her with a family, by how many contrivances must she win their love and affection; with what solicitude must she keep far away from them every occasion of evil, and with what perseverance must she inure their young minds to virtue! The vigilance exercised over them in a religious community; the examples of virtue which they see around them; the spirit of regularity and religion which they almost unconsciously imbibe in it, are eminently calculated to fit them for this high office, which they are to exercise. The effects of this salutary discipline may be seen in the models of every domestic excellence and religious virtue which the Ursuline community has given to society in so many of its pupils.

Besides the schools for the education of the wealthier classes, which formed the more immediate object of this institute, and which were soon filled by boarders from all parts of the kingdom, the members were not unmindful of the instruction of the poor. They took under their immediate care and management, the poor schools which Miss Nagle had previously conducted; and to this day there is a school for the instruction of poor children attached to most convents of the order. But they had not been long in Cork when dangers began to gather round them, and the worst apprehensions which were entertained for their security seemed about to be realized. The no-Popery corporation of the day, which had so long viewed with indifference the turbulence and·outrages which were occurring within the city, became indignant at such a violation of law, as the establishment of a

Popish nunnery.   They resolved on getting rid at once of such a
stain on its Protestantism and its loyalty.   They assembled a full
court of D'Oyer Hundred, as it was termed, to consider on the
most effectual means by which the nuisance might be removed.
The meagre and imperfect records of the time do not say how
many plans of extermination were recommended and discussed
then.   They had not the example of enlightened Boston, to
teach them the best and quickest way of getting rid of a convent.
But it is certain, that some violent measure was in contemplation,
and would have been adopted, but for the interference of one
influential member of the name of Carleton.   His name deserves
to be mentioned with honour.   He restrained their intolerant
and anti-Catholic propensities, by appealing to a principle more
powerful with them than humanity or religion—their own
pecuniary interests.   It would be more beneficial for themselves,
he said, and for the city, to have the money of these ladies and
their pupils expended at home, than to force them by persecution, to go and live elsewhere.   And he good-humouredly added,
that he saw no very imminent danger to the Protestant religion,
or the Protestant succession in the meeting of a few old ladies
to take their tea and say their prayers together of an evening.
The influence of the individual, as well, perhaps, as the good
sense of the advice, prevailed over the bigotry of the body.
The purposes of intolerance were defeated.   Constant residence
reconciled the Protestants to their presence among them, and
constant experience demonstrated their utility to the public.
But such was the insecurity of their position, and so feeble the
thread by which they held their freedom from molestation, that
for years they dared not assume the religious habit, except on
solemn festivals, and in the veriest privacy of the convent.   It
was not until the 11th of November, 1779, and even then in
opposition to the prudent though timid remonstrances of their
friends, that they laid aside the secular dress for good, and
assumed the ordinary costume of their order.   The issue proved
that the apprehensions of their friends were excessive.   Other

and better times came gradually on. They shared in the increasing rights and privileges of their people; and the daughters of St. Ursula have never since been molested.

With the exception of Mrs. Kelly, there was as yet no professed nun in the convent. To effect this important object, a bull was procured from Pope Clement XIV., dated January 13th, 1773, permitting the first twelve novices to be professed after one year's probation, thus dispensing, in their regard, with one-half of the usual and prescribed term of noviciate. Availing themselves of this permission, the sisters, Angela Fitzsimons, Joseph Nagle, and Ursula Kavanagh, were professed on the 15th of the following February. Miss Coppinger, who had been obliged by the state of her health to retire to the country for a time, returned, and after a year's noviciate, was professed on the 21st December, as was also, on the 26th of April, 1774, Miss Moylan. The latter could have availed herself of the permission of Clement, but she preferred the full term of noviciate prescribed by the constitution of the order. Their number was still further increased by the profession of Miss Daly, on the 4th July, and Miss Stack, on the 29th of the following September. There being now seven professed religious in the young community, exclusive of Mrs. Kelly and the novices, it was thought expedient to organize its internal system and management, according to the form prescribed by the rule. Accordingly, on the 31st January, 1775, was held the first chapter of the Institute in Ireland. The community having thus acquired some stability, and being established on a secure basis, Mrs. Kelly deemed her mission in this country fulfilled. She was Irish by birth, but Ireland was not the land of her affections. She had resided abroad since her childhood, and the ties were stronger that bound her to " La belle France," than to the green hills of her native country. The quiet tenor of her little convent at Dieppe, contrasted strongly with the bustle and active duties of her new position, and with the insecurity and danger in which they were occasionally placed by the bigotry of the times.

In the Easter of 1775, she returned to her own convent, after an absense of four years. It was a source of much consolation in her declining years, to have been intrumental in conferring so great a blessing on her people. On her departure, the sisters assembled to elect a Mother Superior, and the choice fell on Mrs. Augustine Coppinger, who had been nearly two years a professed religious, and was one of the four who had been in training at St. Jacques. This election took place on the 4th September. Their long-tried and efficient friend, Dr. Moylan, who had been a month or two before consecrated Bishop of Kerry, was present on the occasion.

The Ursulines continued their labours in the house which had been provided for them by Miss Nagle. Nothing occurred to disturb the quiet tenor of their lives, unless when some new accession was received to their number, or when some sister was summoned to her final reward. Of those who contributed to the foundation, Mrs. Mary Joseph Nagle was the first who departed, and she died on the 23rd November, 1789. Mrs. Fitzsimons died on the 25th April, 1801, and Mrs. Ursula Kavanagh on the 18th September, 1804. Mrs. Coppinger's life was prolonged to the 16th November, 1822.

The convent which they occupied being found very inadequate to the purpose, and very insufficient for their wants, it was determined to look out for some more eligible situation, about the year 1820. In the beautiful environs of Cork it was not difficult to find a spot that possessed all the required conditions, and accordingly a beautiful and commodious residence was purchased at Blackrock, a village about two miles from that city, and picturesquely situated on the banks of the river Lee. It had formerly been the property of Mr. Joseph Nagle, and was, in the last century, the residence of 'Henry Sheares, whose connexion with the events of 1798, and melancholy fate, are well known. The first stone of the new buildings were laid on Whitsunday, 9th June, 1824, by the Right Rev. Dr. Murphy, bishop of the diocese, and the removal of the entire community took place on the 12th of October, 1825.

The fruits of the Ursuline community of Cork attracted the attention of that great and good prelate, Dr. James Butler, Archbishop of Cashel. He determined on establishing a branch of the order in Thurles; and for that purpose, Miss Luby commenced her noviciate in Cork, in the year 1787, and when it expired began the new foundation, in the immediate vicinity of the archiepiscopal residence. It had many difficulties to contend with in the early years of its existence. In the year 1818, it was resolved to build a new convent, and the first stone was laid by Dr. Everard, in that year. Since then its career has been one of varying vicissitude. Within the last few years it has received a fresh and vigorous impulse from the zeal of his Grace the present Archbishop, the Most Rev. Dr. Leahy. He had the good fortune to procure, from the parent house in Cork, the services of one of its most gifted members, Mrs. Mary Teresa Joseph Grene. Under her judicious care and most persevering and indefatigable labours, the convent has assumed a new form, and begun a fresh career of public usefulness. New buildings have been erected, spacious and elegant accommodation provided, pupils assembled in considerable numbers, and the progress made most gratifying to every one who has the interests of religion and his country at heart. The prospects of this community are most promising. The railway, which passes close to the town, makes it accessible to persons from every part of the kingdom, and its central position and other advantages, combine to render it one of the most convenient educational establishments of the kingdom. In the year 1816, it was proposed to erect a convent of this institute in Waterford. The new community arrived in that city on the first day of August in that year. Not finding their first residence in Waterpark suited to their purposes, they removed after a short time to a place called Newgrove; and finally, in October, 1824, to their present convent at St. Mary's. It is prettily situated about a mile from the city, and though within reach of its practical advantages, it is yet completely separated from the bustle of a populous and busy neighbourhood. On the 26th of June the first religious profession took place in this convent.

In the year 1826, a branch of the Ursulines was founded in Limerick, but not meeting with the expected success, it was removed to Galway. After some time it was transferred to Athlone.

Two foundations were made in America, one in the city of New York in the year, 1812, and the other in Charleston, South Carolina, in the year 1834. The first was dissolved in the course of a few years, and the second will scarcely survive the calamities in which Charleston is involved in the present war.

PRESENTATION NUNS.

In tracing, consecutively, the events that led to the establishment of the Ursulines, Miss Nagle has for the time been lost sight of. It has been already observed, that the object dearest to her heart, and for which she made such generous sacrifices, was the education of the poor. When the new order was introduced, that object seemed secured. She was therefore disappointed, that, by their institute, her views were not carried out as fully as she intended. That institute was for the rich rather than the poor. If these were to come under its care, and share in the blessings it conferred, it was but in a subordinate degree, and their claims were but secondary to those of the others. Their interests were not neglected indeed, but they were not the great and primary object of attention. She believed her mission to be to the poor and the humble, and she could not be supposed to witness with pleasure an arrangement so unfavourable to them.

She wished, as may be perceived by her letters, that the new colony should be instructed, and qualified in all respects to teach even the wealthier classes such departments of knowledge as their condition required; but she never contemplated it principally for them. She remonstrated against this deviation from her original intentions; and when her remonstrance was unavailing, she retired from the convent, for she had actually taken up her abode within it. The object which Miss Nagle disapproved, was, by the very words of their constitution, a primary object of their institute, and could not be altered. It was not to the community itself that she had any objection, for she ever remained on terms of the most friendly intercourse with the sisters, and during the remaining years of her life was accustomed to visit their schools for an hour on Saturdays, to give religious instruction to the children. It was not that she did not love their institute well, but she would have loved another better. It is to be regretted that on a matter of such importance there should have been any misapprehension, and that a clear and definite understanding was not come to during the three years that the business was in progress. Perhaps she thought that the Ursuline institute, whatever it may have been in France, would, under the pressure of circumstances in Ireland, accommodate itself to the purposes she had more immediately in view, and in which she believed it could be made more useful. From a comparison of all the facts, it seems highly probable that this last is the probable solution. But whatever was the cause, it has had a very beneficial influence on religion in this country. It is but one of the many instances in which Providence orders all things sweetly and for the best and wisest ends, and in which, to use the words of the holy A Kempis, " Man proposes, but God disposes." On the shifting tide of human events there are influences at work, and movements in progress, passing the comprehension as they escape the notice of those who live and move upon the surface. And such was the institution of the Ursulines. Without such an order, the Presentation, or any institute having for its sole object

the education of the poor, would have been impossible. There
was not in Ireland at that time, as in France and other countries
an educated upper or middle class to furnish subjects qualified
by their attainments and education for its efficient management.
It is not the uneducated that are to do the work of education.
This would be setting the blind to teach the blind. The germ
of knowledge must be brought to maturity in one mind before
it can be communicated profitably to another, for the seed that is
sown unripened will never bud forth or fructify. The education of the poor requires a regular and abundant supply of those
who are themselves educated; and to obtain such in Ireland, where
the springs of knowledge had been for years dried up, was until
then impossible. They had to be created; and some institute was
necessary to supply that knowledge which only a favoured few
could acquire abroad. This object the Ursulines accomplished.
They prepared the way, and furnished the agents, in the great
work of the enlightenment and education of the poor children of
this country. Even to this day a considerable portion of the
members of the Presentation order are indebted to it for their
education, and, perhaps, for their vocation to a religious life;
and however it may have been originally opposed to the wishes
of its foundress, it was an important, if not an essential instrument, in effecting the objects which she so ardently and earnestly
had in view.

Thus disappointed in the hope which had sustained her
through many a long year of anxious expectancy, she yet does
not abandon her object in despair. An humble but firm trust
in the providence of God, supports her in one more effort in the
cause that was so dear to her. She took up her abode in a house
adjoining the convent, and was joined by a few generous individuals, animated with the same spirit as herself. Her
pecuniary means were not all exhausted by the efforts she had
already made, and she was therefore able to make a permanent
and adequate provision for their support. This establishment
was the germ of the Presentation order. She herself had always

a tender devotion to the Presentation of our Blessed Lady in the Temple, and she wished that her little society should be distinguished by that title. They were to make annual vows, and to form nothing more than a simple religious society. Their vocation and duty were, like hers, to seek out the poor girls of the city; to gather them around them; to teach them the rudiments of knowledge; to instil into their minds the principles of religion; to relieve their wants by supplying them with the few articles of food and clothing which their necessities required; and, if possible, to provide them with some means of subsistence for the future. They were to subject themselves to no law of enclosure, for the comprehensive charity of Miss Nagle would have them visit the poor man's hovel and the sick man's bed. It was said of her, that she left not a garret in Cork unvisited. Everywhere her footsteps were to be traced, equally in the filthiest lane, and the lowliest cottage. Like Him whom she loved so well and ardently, she went about everywhere doing good. Such were the high duties which she wished her associates to fulfil; and they did fulfil them, not only during her lifetime, but for years after her death. In troubled times they performed all the useful and meritorious duties which are now discharged by the Sisters of Mercy and Charity. The children of the poor were educated; the sick and the indigent visited both in their houses and in the public hospitals. Enclosure within the walls of their convents would have been incompatible with these objects, and therefore was not observed. The services they rendered to religion were so manifest, and such a provision for the moral and religious wants of the people so loudly called for, that in a few years it was extended to several other towns in Ireland.

The new institute was commenced by Miss Nagle towards the close of the year 1777, and the house was opened on Christmas day in that year. This event was marked by a singular instance of her affection for the suffering children of her Redeemer. Fifty indigent persons were entertained by her at table, and ministered to with her own hands. She continued during her life to repeat this charity on each recurrence of that festival; and it is said, that the same duty is still performed in the parent house of the Presentation order. This was but one of the many actions in which she was employed. During the thirty years of her mission, for such it may be called, her career of charity was scarcely interrupted for a day. Morning, noon, and night she was ever occupied in her kind and charitable duties, breaking the bread of life to the ignorant, or the meat which perisheth to the hungry. Her solicitude extended even to the youth of the other sex. It has been already mentioned, that she provided from the very beginning a school for the instruction of boys. She provided an alms-house for the aged and decrepid female poor, which is still in existence. The last work of charity in which she was employed, was an asylum for penitent females; but this design she did not live to accomplish. She would receive and shelter, were it necessary, in her bosom, the wretched outcasts at whom the very world, which has made them what they are, points the finger of scorn and abhorrence. This merciful and benevolent design she would most assuredly have carried into effect, if her destined career of usefulness was not already at an end, and her measure of good works filled up, pressed down, and already running over.

But the goodness of God's chosen servants does not consist in works of charity alone. The beauty of the king's daughter is chiefly from within; and though from the fulness of the heart the mouth speaketh, and the hand worketh, yet there are hidden trials reserved for the children of God, which the world often can never know. It is only He who calls them and sustains them in the conflict, and makes with the temptation issue, that knows how steep and rugged, and strewed with many a trial, is the secret path by which the soul is led upwards to perfection, and prepared for glory. Miss Nagle, like the servants of God in every age, had her internal trials. Beside her daily solicitude, like the Apostle, for her numerous children, she had on many occasions to encounter contradiction and disappointment, and what is yet worse, insult and contumely. She was more than once called an impostor and a hypocrite in the public streets, and she heard her benevolence condemned as reckless extravagance, and her piety as pharisaical ostentation. She had to suffer from the corrupt malignity of her enemies; for even the best and holiest will have enemies. But, like Him, who, when reviled, did not revile, and who, when led like a sheep to the slaughter, opened not His mouth, her only reply was silence and uncomplaining submission. The barbed arrow pierced her bosom, but no one knew of the wound that it inflicted, nor would they have known it, if a considerate solicitude for her spiritual daughters did not lead her to put them on their guard against the wiles of the tempter, and fortify their inexperienced minds against the virulent aspersions of calumny. So lowly was the estimate she formed of herself, and the joy she experienced in any involuntary occasion of humiliation, that she preserved, as a cherished relic, an alms which she received one day at the door of her convent. The gentleman who gave it did not know her, but thought that one so poor and humble, yet so resigned, pious, and unpretending in her demeanour, must be an object worthy of his charity. She usually spent four hours every morning in prayer. She made each year a spiritual retreat of eight days, great part of which she spent in the church on bended knees; and the night of Holy Thursday was ever with her one of sacred and uninterrupted watching before the adorable Sacrament of the Altar. After death her knees were found excoriated, and in part ulcerated, and they must have been so for years; yet the acute and piercing agony which kneeling must have caused her, she bore with the most enduring fortitude. She never whispered to her nearest and dearest associates a hint of this secret and long-continued suffering, which was known but to herself and God. There were large tumours, too, on the soles of her feet, so that the wonder was that she was able to walk at all. And yet, for the last three years of her life, she travelled over great part of the city, seeking from door to door the means of support for those many charitable foundations which would otherwise have fallen to the ground.

Such was the tenor of Miss Nagle's life. It was spent in the performance of good works, and in the practice of great virtues. She was ever doing penance for sins of which her profound humility persuaded her she was guilty. In the beginning of 1784 she reached the fifty-sixth year of her age, and in the spring of that year the symptoms of a premature old age began to develop themselves in her exhausted frame. Hers was not the infirmity of years, but of severe and long-protracted labours. She began to complain of weakness, oppression, loss of rest and appetite, and a troublesome cough aggravated not a little the sufferings of the last moments of her life. On the 26th of April it became evident to all around her that her last hour was come. She had previously received the last rites of religion, and calling her little community around her, she gave them her last lesson. It was that which she had taught them during life: " Love one another as you have hitherto done;" and taking her last farewell of them, she passed gently from this world to a better.

Thus died one of the greatest women that has been given to our time, or adorned our country. The world may not be always disposed to think her so, but she was great before God. Her remains lie in the quiet and beautiful little cemetery, formed originally for the Ursulines, but now belonging to the Presentation nuns. Those early associates whom she loved so well are buried by her side. No sound intrudes to break the silent loneliness of the spot, nor step to brush the dew-drops from their graves, except when a spiritual daughter comes to learn a lesson of self-devotion and perseverence at her tomb, or a casual visitor is brought there by the memory of her virtues and her name.

The death of their foundress was a severe affliction to the sisters of the Presentation order. Her example and advice would be of great service to the young community, if God had spared her life for some years longer. But so judicious was the system on which it was established, and so perfect the religious spirit which she infused into it, that the work of charity was continued with undiminished zeal. Her body was in the grave, but her spirit survived, and continued to animate her children. So beneficial were the results of their labours, that the bishops of the neighbouring dioceses desired to share in the blessings enjoyed by the people of Cork, and were anxious that the institute should be extended to other places. As yet it was only a simple society of individuals, aggregated together by mere episcopal authority, but it was deemed advisable to have it approved by the Holy See. Accordingly a request to that effect was transmitted to Rome, and laid before his Holiness Pope Pius VI., who then occupied the chair of Peter. The storm was already gathering, which soon after burst with such dread results on the Church and on society. Its first murmurings were already heard. The struggle had commenced in France. The efforts of an infidel press, and the intrigues of powerful and unprincipled men, had succeeded in embittering the courts of Europe against the religious orders, and in some instances against religion itself. Scarce a day passed without some new and indignant remonstrance against them being presented at the Vatican, from those governments that had hitherto been their most zealous supporters. The Jesuits, powerful and influential as they were, had been already sacrificed to their hostility, and if the doom of others was delayed, it seemed certainly and speedily at hand. At this critical and eventful period it was that the petition on behalf of the sisters of the Presentation was laid before his Holiness, praying that they might be raised to the dignity of a religious institute. It was a balm to the afflicted heart of the pontiff, and a harbinger of other and better times. It was a sure indication that the religious spirit was not dead in Christendom. Though the cauldron was seething with the ingredients of mischief, and the burning waters threatened to inundate the altar and the throne, there was one spot at least on God's earth which was yet green with the dew of heaven, and where grace was producing fruit like that which it produced of old, when the hills were peopled with anchorets, and the valleys were studded with the abodes of learning and religion.

The following is the apostolic brief, addressed to the Right Rev. Francis Moylan, approving of its existence, and authorising its extension to the other towns in Ireland. It is dated the 3rd day of September, 1791, and was wet with the tears of joy which the pontiff shed upon the page:—

" Venerable Brother, health and apostolical benediction.

" In our solicitude for all the Churches, nothing can give us more pleasure than that such opportunities should occur as may enable us to contribute to the spiritual welfare of Christ's faithful servants, and to impart to them, and more particularly to those who live among persons not professing the Catholic faith, the graces and favours of this Holy See, and to direct our whole study, care, and diligence, to instruct and preserve them in the practice of piety and good morals.

" Hence, venerable brother, you will easily conceive the sentiments with which we received your postulation of the following tenor, presented to us by our Sacred Congregation, *de Propaganda Fide*, to which you had addressed it.

" Miss Hanora Nagle, of respectable memory, had determined to employ the ample fortune she possessed in founding houses or communities for the admission of pious virgins, whose principal duty should be to instruct little girls in the rudiments and precepts of the Catholic faith; to teach them to work; to visit the sick women in the public infirmaries, and administer to them spiritual and temporal assistance, &c.

" And whereas there is now, as is represented, a house prepared and fitted for such an establishment in the city of Cork, wherein some have already joined this pious institution, and others are disposed to enter the same, should it receive the approbation of the Apostolical See; in consequence of which you, yourself, venerable brother, sensible of the advantages of so pious an institution, have supplicated us, through the same Congregation, to confirm it. More grateful, indeed, or more seasonable intelligence we could not receive, especially at the present time, when the designs and schemes of wicked men tend to nothing less than the ruin and destruction, were such a thing possible, of the Church of Christ, founded and formed by His precious blood. We feel and acknowledge it an effort of the boundless providence of the Almighty God, that while elsewhere the institutions and convents of the religious of both sexes are sacrilegiously plundered and destroyed, houses are, by the increase of piety in your diocese, erected and endowed for the reception of pious virgins, whereby the Christian education of young girls is happily secured. Having, therefore, first of all, offered due thanks to the divine mercy, and next highly approving in the Lord the aforesaid Hanora Nagle's intentions, sincerely also and earnestly inclined in favour of your petition, with the advice of our venerable brethren, the cardinals of the Holy Roman Catholic Church, charged with the affairs *de Propaganda Fide,* for the greater glory of God and the promotion of religion, we give you, venerable brother, in virtue of our apostolical authority, and by these our present letters in form of brief, power to erect and to form, not only in the city of Cork, but also in other cities, towns, and places of Ireland (taking care, however, always to procure the consent of the ordinary, when there is question of another diocese), one or more houses for the reception of pious virgins, whose duty it shall be to instruct little girls in the rudiments of the Catholic faith and good morals, to teach them different works appropriate to their sex, to visit sick females in public infirmaries, and to help them in their necessities.

" But in order that the aforesaid virgins may perform these works of piety with the greater fruit for the salvation of souls, we will and commend them to observe the rules and constitutions to be made and appointed by you, approaching as near as possible to the institute of St. Ursula, and conformable to the instructions to be transmitted to you by the said Congregation;

and also that, having completed the time of probation, they shall make simple vows, that is, the vows of obedience, chastity, and poverty, and that of persevering in the said holy purpose, from which vows they cannot be released or absolved by any person but by you and your successors in your diocese, and by the other ordinaries in their own, to whose jurisdiction the aforementioned virgins, wherever established, must be subject; and this only for just and reasonable motives approved of by you or by them.

"And that no spiritual help towards the more cheerful and zealous performance of their duties be wanting to the aforesaid virgins, we give and grant unto them, through our apostolical sovereignty, all the same indulgences and spiritual graces hitherto granted by us and our predecessors to the religious of St. Ursula, to their convents and to their churches.

"We beseech our great and good God to give success and increase to this new undertaking; and in order to obtain in its favour His heavenly blessing, we bestow on it our apostolical benediction, which we most affectionately impart to you also, venerable brother, with the most profound sentiments of benevolence and esteem.

"Given at Rome, at St. Mary Major's, under the Fisherman's Ring, the 3rd day of September, 1791, and the 17th of our pontificate.

(Signed,)   " BENEDICT STAY."

Having received the apostolic approval and benediction, it was extended in a few years to several other cities and towns in Ireland; and before the end of the year 1805, there were large and flourishing establishments in Killarney, Waterford, Kilkenny, and Dublin. There had been until then no deviation from the original nature and purpose of the institution. They not only educated the poor, but they visited the sick in the public hospitals and in their own homes. In that year some influential friends thought it would be more advisable, by confining the religious to the enclosure of their convents, to limit their usefulness to the work of education alone. This deviation from its original purpose, and abandonment of one great object contemplated by the foundress of the institute, was the subject of much deliberation, and was disapproved of by many at the time. It has interfered not a little with the extension of the Presentation order to places where its labours are much needed. There can be no doubt that in some circumstances a sub-division of the offices of charity into their respective and separate departments, may be attended with most beneficial results. For, into spiritual concerns, the same principle of a sub-division of labour may be successfully introduced, which has contributed in so eminent a degree to excellence in science and the arts. It must be admitted, that if a community or an order be entrusted with a school alone, it is more likely to attain success therein than if it had the charge of an hospital besides. The more exclusively the mind and the attention are devoted to one object, the sooner and better will it be accomplished. This sub-division of charity may be practicable and advisable in large cities, where there is enough of duty and enough of pecuniary means for all; but it is often impracticable in the smaller towns. It is by much exertion, and with much expense, that a religious establishment, however required, can be formed in a provincial town. It is very seldom that means can be found, or that even a wish is entertained, of establishing a second in the same locality. The one that is established should, in common prudence, be made available for all the spiritual wants of the locality and its inhabitants. The poor children should be educated—the sick should be visited—wretched penitent females should be reclaimed—the children of shopkeepers and persons in wordly circumstances should be also instructed. There is no class, perhaps, so little attended to as the latter. An honest pride prevents them from availing themselves of the gratuitous education of the Presentation schools, and want of means precludes them from the advantages of the Ursulines. They are, consequently, obliged to receive such instruction as a half-educated schoolmaster or mistress in a country town can afford them. When the means of endowment are limited, it would, therefore, be very advisable to make them available for the wants of all. Hence the Presentation order, when limited in its objects, was diminished in its means of usefulness. The wants which it could not remedy had to be provided for in some other way, and the congregations of Charity and Mercy were originated and established. These would, in all probability, never have been thought of, but for the changes introduced into the Presentation institute. If this had remained unaltered, the convents of the order, which are now about fifty in number, would be at least one hundred. Notwithstanding the opposition of some, the purpose of raising the institute to the dignity of a religious order, and thereby enabling its members to make solemn religious vows, was persevered in, and diligently pursued. A code of rules and constitutions was drawn up, at the request of Dr. Moylan, by the Rev. Laurence Callanan, a Franciscan friar, then resident in Cork. They were taken principally from those of the Ursulines, the only difference being such as was required by the different objects of each institute. They were laid before his Holiness Pope Pius VII., in the year 1805, and on the ninth of April in that year he approved of the same, and complied with the object of the petition, in the following brief, addressed, as was the other, to his venerable brother, Francis, Bishop of Cork:—

" Venerable Brother, health and apostolic benediction.

" The care of the pastoral affairs, committed to us from above, which extends to the entire flock of our Lord, requires most particularly of us sedulously to listen to the voice of the pastors, who implore the assistance of the Apostolic See, in order to revive and promote Christian piety in their flocks, and efficiently to unite our exertions with their zeal. It having been represented to us, in your name, that Hanora Nagle, an opulent and noble Catholic lady of the kingdom of Ireland, did employ her fortune in founding houses for the purpose of receiving pious virgins, who are desirous of devoting themselves to the laborious duty of instructing young girls, especially the poor, in the rudiments of the Catholic faith, and in different works suitable to their station; and, likewise, of visiting sick females in the public infirmaries, and administering to their spiritual and temporal relief; and whereas some have already joined this charitable institution, and many more have shown an earnest desire of embracing the same, if it should be approved of by the Apostolical See; and whereas our late predecessor, Pius VI., granted to you, by his apostolic letters, &c., the faculty of erecting, not only in the city of Cork, but also in the other towns of Ireland, houses for the reception of those who are desirous of employing themselves in the aforesaid works of charity, and who, after completing the time of their probation, are to make simple vows of obedience, poverty, and chastity. Wonderful, indeed, does the rapid and successful increase of that institution appear after receiving the apostolic approbation, and not less so the multiplied and abundant fruit it has produced, wherever established, since it flourishes now not only in the city of Cork, but has extended itself also to the counties of Dublin, Waterford, Kilkenny, and the town of Killarney. But what is of still greater consequence, not only young girls, but also the adult, and even married women, frequent these communities, to learn what they are generally ignorant of—the principles of faith and morals—insomuch, that the pious virgins, already professing that institute, have rejoiced at the visible increase of religion; and being more anxiously desirous of its further progress, unanimously and earnestly have solicited to be converted into real religious, and to be consecrated by solemn vows, for the education and instruction of young females, particularly the poor, which consideration, it appears to you, would tend considerably to the stability and perfection of this institution, and contribute also to fix therein, with greater attachment, those virgins, so animated with zeal for the glory of God. Whereas, then, the said Pius, our predecessor, in order that these virgins might, with greater alacrity of spirit, embrace their duties, did most abundantly impart to them all the indulgences and spiritual favours already granted to the religious of the order of St. Ursula, and did impose on you the obligation of composing for them rules similar to those of the institute of St. Ursula, which, being now completed by you with the utmost care, and strengthened by the weighty suffrages of other ordinaries of the kingdom, and after being, with most mature deliberation, examined by the cardinals, have lately been laid before us of the following tenor.

[Here follow the rules at full length.]

" Whereupon you have humbly prayed us to approve of those rules, and to grant, through our apostolical benignity, to the said virgins, the favour of being transferred from the state of members of a simple congregation to that of real religious, under the title and invocation of the Presentation of the Blessed Virgin Mary : we, therefore, are desirous of seconding your zeal, and the wishes of the aforesaid virgins, in a matter that so nearly concerns the glory of God and the increase of religion; willing also to confer on you and them our special favours and graces, we approve of these rules and constitutions, with all and everything contained in them ; we consider and declare them ratified and valid, and superadd to them the force of perpetual and inviolable stability ; we consent and grant to the now existing virgins, and to all future ones, that they may and can, on the expiration of the time of probation, having observed all that is otherwise to be observed, be admitted to the solemn profession of religious vows, with the addition of a fourth, namely, that of educating and instructing young girls, especially the poor, in the precepts and rudiments of the Catholic faith, in such ways, nevertheless, as that they be obliged in future to live under these rules, to be subject to the jurisdiction of the ordinary, to observe the laws of enclosure; and, therefore, never, by any means, to pass the limits of the monastery, unless for the reasons sanctioned by the canon law. For which reason, as far as it may be necessary, we expressly dispense with the obligation before mentioned—of visiting sick women in the infirmaries; and in this point, we derogate from the letters of our predecessor. Moreover, we confirm all the indulgences and spiritual favours granted by him to this institution.

"Given at Rome, in the sixth year of our pontificate.
"(Signed)
"G. Berni, Deputy for Cardinal Braschi Onesti."

The words of this brief have been, in some passages, condensed; the sense has, however, been scrupulously preserved. The constitutions are, everywhere, replete with maxims of the highest religious perfection. The greater part of them relate to duties, the internal economy, and government of the religious themselves. The following paragraphs, from the first and second chapters, contain all that is most immediately interesting to the public:—

"1.—Besides their own perfection and sanctification—which is the great end of all religious orders—the sisters admitted into this congregation must also, and especially, have in view the instruction of poor female children in the principles of religion and piety. In this arduous and meritorious undertaking, they shall encourage themselves, and animate their zeal and fervour by the example of their Divine Master, who always testified the tenderest love for little children, expressed the greatest pleasure in their approaching Him, and declares, ' whosoever receiveth those little ones in His name receiveth Him.' They shall also consider, that in cultivating the tender minds of young children, by infusing into them a horror of vice and a love of virtue, and by instructing them in the duties of religion, they are associated to the functions of those heavenly spirits, whom God has appointed guardian angels, to watch over and direct them in the ways of eternal salvation.

"2.—They shall teach the children daily the catechism,

explaining it to them briefly and simply, in language adapted
to their age and capacity. They shall not propose anything
abstruse, that might embarrass either the children or themselves.
They shall accustom them to think, and speak with reverence
of God and holy things, and not to be ever curious in their
questions, but constantly exhort them to captivate their understanding in obedience to faith, keeping their minds always disposed to receive instruction from those whom Christ has
appointed to rule the Church of God, which He purchased with
His blood.

" 3.—They shall teach the children to offer themselves up
to God, from the first use of reason; and when they awake in
the morning, to raise their hearts to Him, to adore His Sovereign
Majesty, return Him thanks for all His favours, and arm themselves with the sign of the cross. They shall instruct them
how they are to offer up all their thoughts, words, and actions
to God's glory, implore His grace to know and love Him, and
to fulfil His commandments, and how they are to examine
their consciences every night, and honour and respect their
parents.

" 4.—They shall teach them how to prepare for confession,
and to confess their sins with all sincerity and contrition.
They shall be ever attentive to prepare them for the sacrament
of Confirmation, and also for their first Communion.

" 5.—As the poor are the main object and particular end of
this pious institute, it is hereby enacted, as a statute inviolably
to be observed, that the sisters shall admit none into their
schools but poor children, nor can they receive money, or any
other temporal emolument for instruction, contenting themselves
with the glorious retribution, promised to those ' who instruct
many to justice.'

" 6.—The sisters appointed by the mother-superior to attend
the schools, shall, with all zeal, charity, and humility, purity of
intention, and confidence in God, undertake the charge, and
cheerfully submit to every labour and fatigue annexed thereto,

mindful of their vocation, and of the glorious recompense attached to the faithful discharge of their duty.

" 7.—When the mistresses enter the schools, they shall raise up their hearts to God, and to the Queen of heaven, and then salute with all reverence, interiorly, the guardian angels of the children, recommending themselves and the dear little ones to their care and protection. They shall endeavour to inspire the children with a sincere devotion to the passion of Jesus Christ, to His real presence in the most holy sacrament, to the immaculate Mother of God, and to their guardian angels.

" 8.—The scholars in each school shall be divided into classes of ten or twelve, according to their total number, and in every class the mistress shall appoint one of the most advanced and most regular scholars as a superintendent, to watch over the others, to keep them in order, make them give an account of their lessons and catechism, inform her of the absentees, and acquaint her of any impropriety they may be guilty of either in or out of school.

" 9.—In each school there shall be a register of the names and ages of the children at the time of entrance, the names and occupations of their parents, their place of abode, and the date of the children's being received into the school.

" 10.—They shall be taught reading, writing, needlework, and spinning. The hours of school shall be, in the morning, from nine to twelve and a quarter, and in the evening from one to half-past three. At a quarter before twelve, silence shall be observed, to accustom the children to recollect themselves in the presence of God, and to afford the sisters the opportunity of making their particular examen. Then the Angelus Domini, with the Acts of Contrition, Faith, Hope, and Charity, shall be said. Half an hour before school breaks up in the evening, a spiritual lecture shall be delivered to the children, out of some instructive book suited to their capacity, or a meditation not above their understanding, in order thus to forward and direct them in true and solid piety. The books chosen for this purpose

H

shall be approved of by the Ordinary. After this they shall pray for the benefactors of the institute, and say the Rosary or Litany of the Blessed Virgin, to recommend themselves to her holy protection.

" 11.—The schools shall be kept as clean and as airy as possible. The mother-superior or her assistants shall visit them at least once a week. There shall be vacation from the schools on all Saturdays, and from the feast of our Blessed Lady of Mount Carmel, until the Monday after the octave of the feast of her Assumption; and from the 20th of December until the Monday immediately after New Year's Day, and from Wednesday in Holy Week until the Monday after Low Sunday, on every holiday of obligation, and on the eve and feast of the Presentation of our Blessed Lady.

" 12.—On the days of vacation, and whenever the sisters are disengaged from the schools, they shall be always ready to instruct in their prayers, and the different mysteries of religion, such poor ignorant women as may be recommended to them by the parochial clergy."

There can be but one opinion on the important influence which such an institute is likely to exercise on the people of a country. The Christian spirit which breathes through every page of these rules and constitutions, and the minute accuracy with which the details of the various duties are prescribed, have produced the best results. Their educational labours have been most successful. The zeal of the teachers is not kept alive by any selfish and mercenary motive, for they are led to the performance of their duties by the high motive of charity alone. What they do they do for God. In each of the upturned little faces, that looks to them for instruction, they see an immortal soul entrusted to their care, and for whose salvation they are to be responsible. The voice of religion tells them, that angels are ever hovering round them, noting every exertion for their improvement, and taking deep interest in the progress of those who have been assigned to their special guardianship. Hence arises a certainty of their interests being attended to, greater than any earthly guarantee can afford, and by a class and description of teachers, such as in any other circumstances they could never have, and whose manners and acquirements are eminently calculated to improve them. The tie which binds the religious to her pupils is of no common order. It partakes more of the parent than the mistress. She becomes the depository of their little wants, cares, and domestic trials. The word of kindness when the child is good—of friendly caution when wayward and unruly—of substantial aid when in poverty and distress, bind them in a close and mutual attachment, which endures for many a year, after the school has been exchanged for the cares and duties of the world. In prosperity, it cheers with the consciousness of her approval; in misfortune, with the hope of sympathy. Even in those darker vicissitudes of sin and shame, which often are the lot of the poor man's daughter, however well-instructed she may have previously been, it has on more than one occasion been the means by which they have been brought back to religion and to God. The heart that was first giving way to despair, becomes softened once more with salutary sentiments of compunction, when she is led by some kind and charitable friend to see her former mistress. The words of one who, in her younger days, was ever wont to speak kindly to her, and to form so tenderly her lips to say prayers—prayers which she has not, alas! repeated for many a year—and who was wont to tell her what she should do, when she encountered the dangers of the world; the words of one whom, in spite of all her own errors and crimes, she still finds kind, and charitable, and forgiving as ever, have often effected, in the reformation of character, what few other means were capable of doing.

Beside the convents in Ireland, there is one in Manchester, one in Madras, and some in Newfoundland. In the wide sphere of usefulness and present prosperity of the institute, may be discerned the care of a special and protecting Providence. As it was the Spirit of God that suggested its establishment in the beginning, so that Spirit has since guided its progress, and blessed its labours. Its extension is a remarkable proof that the Catholic is a living faith, capable of great and wondrous things, even in the most unfavourable circumstances. The progress of the Presentation order is one fruit of that living and enduring energy, which was imparted to Catholicity by Him who was Himself the truth and the life. The spreading vine and the grain of mustard-seed of the Gospel were its types. Its fruits may be seen in the religious orders and charitable foundations of every age and clime, and is still in active operation in the pervading and benevolent spirit of modern Catholicism. It may be checked, modified, or for a time suppressed by human power, but it can never be utterly destroyed; for, like Him from whom it emanated, it is immortal and indestructible. The Presentation institute was not supported by missionary societies, nor brought into public notice by the agency of the public press, nor placed beyond the reach of failure by Royal or Parliamentary munificence. It had to work its way unnoticed, shunning, as far as possible, the observation of the world, and seen but by those who felt its generous protection, and who, by its holy agency, were instructed unto justice. It was a living and healthy branch of that true vine, whose roots were fixed deep in the everlasting hills, and which has, ere now, withstood the storms of persecution, and been productive of much extensive good. The portion of God's vineyard in which it flourished seemed, in the inscrutable ways of Providence, to have been abandoned to desolation. The wild beasts of the forest were permitted to waste and ravage it for a season. Stormy and troubled days they were in which it was planted, but it put forth its leaves, and blossomed, and bore fruit an hundredfold, for it was one which the right hand of the Lord had planted. How little fruit has Protestantism produced, although it has had kings for its nursing-fathers, and queens for its nursing-mothers! How few voices have issued from deanery or vicarage, from collegiate walls or episcopal palace, to call together the children of the poor, and, in the power of a common Christian brotherhood, to lead them, by word and example and winning encouragement, to their Father who is in heaven! Have the towns of Manchester, Sheffield, Birmingham, Leeds, or London, heard wisdom crying aloud in the streets, and, with a mother's love, calling the neglected children of the poor, from lane and factory, to taste the sweets of religion and knowledge, until the Catholic Church was established in the midst of their people? If the mother's heart be known by its instinctive love, tenderness, and solicitude for her children, who has proved herself the mother of the poor?

How favourably does the Presentation institute contrast with the Charter Schools of Ireland, which, at the very time that Miss Nagle was engaged in her own sphere of usefulness, received so much of royal favour and legislative endowment! How different has been the fruit, how different the result of the two! The history of Charter Schools has been one tissue of fraud, peculation, and mismanagement; and if we were to use the words of the official report presented to Government, its fruits would be expressed in language which shall not be named. Vast sums of money were expended upon them, and they were under the especial care of the Established Church of Ireland; yet, in comparatively few years, they became such nuisances, that the very power which founded was compelled to remove them from the country for ever. The Presentation institute, on the other hand, goes on increasing in public usefulness and favour, winning for itself golden opinions from all men and from all parties; producing results such as, with similar, or far greater means, Protestantism has not produced. Yet this was the work of one lady, in one of the most misgoverned countries of the earth, and with many social, legal, and political obstacles to encounter. If England has nothing like it now to show, it was not so in the Catholic times of old, when she was connected with the centre of unity, from which alone the living principle can emanate. Rich and abundant were the fruits which it then bore; its monuments are still to be seen, the mere husk and rind of what these institutions were once. The life is no longer there, because the branch has been severed from its parent stem. It bears the curse of sterility; and until it be engrafted in the true vine, which is Christ Jesus, by being reconciled and united to the centre of Christian unity, it will never bloom nor bud forth again. To use the words of the Irish poet, it lies—

> " Like a dead leafless branch in the summer's bright ray :
> The beams of the warm sun play round it in vain ;
> It may smile in his light, but it blooms not again."

SISTERS OF MERCY.

The order of the Sisters of Mercy is now well known over the world. Of late years its services have been extended to many cities and towns, not only in Ireland, but also in England and America. Yet of those who have been benefited or edified by the exalted virtues for which it is conspicuous, very many are not acquainted even with the name of the great and holy woman to whom that order owes its existence. And yet the circumstances in which it originated, and the means by which, in the designs of Providence, it was brought to its present and prosperous condition, are full of the deepest interest and instruction.

Miss Catherine M'Auley was born on the 17th of September, 1778, at Stormanstown House, in the county of Dublin. She was the eldest of a family of three children. At a very early age she had the misfortune of losing her father, who was a truly religious and edifying Catholic, though he lived at a time when the practical exercise of religion was far from being as general as it has since become. She was old enough to remember that on Sundays and festivals he was wont to collect around him the poor boys and girls of his neighbourhood, for the purpose of instructing them, in his own homely and impressive manner, in the great truths and duties of religion. His wife, who was very much a woman of the world, had no great liking for such employment, and often remonstrated on what she considered the unsuitableness of such an occupation to a man of his age and condition. But no opposition or entreaty of hers could induce him to abandon the good work in which he volunteered, and which he felt to be attended with great advantages. If the religious instruction of the poor be even in our days a work of such decided utility, and sometimes, even with all the means that the charity of individuals and institutions have provided for the purpose, of such decided necessity, how much more necessary and meritorious must it have been when the religious institutions of the country were then only in their infancy, or were just beginning to emerge from the pressure of those restrictions to which the intolerance of centuries had subjected them! The poor children in the vicinity of Stormanstown House suffered a great and irreparable loss, and must have been overwhelmed with a proportionate affliction, when it pleased God, in the mysterious dispensations of His providence, to deprive them of their good friend and benefactor; and greater still must have been the affliction of his own young family, when, at an early age, the death of that dear, good father made them orphans. Their extreme youth, which perhaps diminished their sense of the affliction, yet made it certainly the more calamitous. Catherine was the only one of his three children who was of an age to really feel the loss; and, in after life, she always cherished the most grateful recollection of his Christian worth, and the most hallowed veneration for his memory. After his death, she, with her sister Mary and her brother James, then almost an infant, were taken by their mother to Dublin. The latter survived her husband but a short time; and when she, too, was taken away from them, they became orphans indeed. A Protestant gentleman, of the name of Armstrong, who had the charge of the Apothecary's Hall, in Mary-street, in that city, and who was, probably, some connexion, or, at least, a friend of the family, took compassion on them, and assumed the care and responsibility of their education. Whatever pecuniary means they had were invested in that establishment, and the revenue that accrued therefrom was applied as a provision for their instruction and subsistence. In their new position they seem to have been amply supplied with everything that their worldly wants required; but their guardian, whether from any indifference of his own on such an important subject, or not wishing to interfere with the children of Catholic parents, took no interest in their religious instruction, and made no provision for that, the most important and essential obligation of those that devolve on persons to whom the guardianship of youth is intrusted. Thus brought up—in the midst of a Protestant family; completely separated from all intercourse with the members of the persuasion to which they belonged; hearing, day after day, the usual misrepresentations of its rites and practices; and with no opportunity of having such misrepresentations removed, or their prejudices corrected—the results may be easily conjectured. The brother, James, adopted the creed of those with whom he lived. His sister, Mary, lost, by degrees, most of the Catholic impressions that were made upon her mind in childhood; and, having married a Protestant gentleman, of the name of M'Cawley, a surgeon in the army, she gave up the few that remained to the requirements of her conjugal affection. Catherine, the eldest, having been more perfectly imbued with Catholic principles, or, at least, having more of Catholic feeling, though she knew little of its truths or practices, was more proof against the influences to which she was subjected. A Protestant she was not; but yet she could scarcely be called a Catholic. She had received little Catholic instruction, and seldom, if ever, was present at a place of Catholic worship. The memory of her beloved father, and her veneration for his virtues, would now and then come strongly on her mind, to sustain her in her trials, and endear to her the faith of which he was a member; but such a sentiment, however it may have encouraged her to persevere in external profession, could not have produced conviction in her mind, and she grew up to the age of womanhood without any settled or decided religious opinions. If, indeed, a remark was made in her presence injurious to the Catholic religion, it always gave her pain, though she knew not in what manner to refute it; and the misrepresentations to which she was often forced to listen, were always to her the source of inward and scarcely suppressed indignation. In this state of doubt and anxiety she remained several years, during her residence in the house of Mr. Armstrong.

Feeling, however, every day, the want of some spiritual assistance, and the necessity of some external guide to conduct her in the way of salvation, she resolved to try whether, by her own study and examination, she could determine which of the two religious communions had the most cogent arguments in its favour, and to which she could, with most safety, commit the guidance and guardianship of her spiritual interests. Having a sincere affection for the persons with whom she lived, and who had always treated her with uniform kindness and attention, she wished to try whether it would be possible, with a safe conscience, to conform to their religious opinions; she read their books, heard their explanations, discussed with them the several points on which they differed, and sought anxiously, by long and deliberate reflection, to persuade herself that the Protestant religion was one which she could, with a safe conscience, embrace. But, alas! the more she read and reflected upon the subject, the stronger her doubts became. The political and worldly motives to which the various forms of Protestantism were indebted for their origin—the violence, contradictions, and mutual dissensions, that marked the conduct of their authors, and the want of those salutary ordinances

H 2

which the experience of her own heart told her were necessary
for spiritual improvement, combined to prove that the spirit
which prompted the Reformation, and animated the Reformers,
could not have been the Spirit of God.

Whatever inclination she may at any time have felt to enrol
herself among its members, utterly died away within her in the
progress of the inquiry. Baffled and disappointed in her efforts
in that direction, at length her mind turned to the consideration of the Catholic doctrines. She procured some books, and
read them with the most serious and profound attention. She
had always cherished a secret partiality for the religion of her
parents, and, therefore, was rejoiced to find that the objections
which had so frequently been urged against it, in her hearing,
had their source in ignorance or misrepresentation of its dogmas.
Having, naturally, a strong instinctive yearning to devotional
observance, she found, to her great delight, that her most
sanguine desires in this respect admitted of being realized. The
antiquity of the Catholic Church, which she was able, so easily,
to trace back to the apostolic times; the universality of its
diffusion, which marked it out as the only Church that fulfilled
the divine injunction of teaching and baptizing the nations; and
the holiness of its devotional practices, which were calculated
to realize the highest degree of her devotional aspirations, made
on her the strongest and most favourable impression, and dis-
pelled those shades of doubt that hitherto obscured her religious
tendencies. In mind and heart she was already a Catholic,
and she only waited for a favourable opportunity of carrying her
resolutions into practice. This did not present itself so soon as
she wished for or expected.

About that time some changes took place in the establishment with which her guardian was connected. Mr. Callaghan,
a gentleman of much eminence in his profession, and of considerable scientific attainments, was appointed head lecturer.
He was but a short time returned from India, where he had
realized a considerable fortune. His office brought him into

frequent intercourse with Mr. Armstrong, and he and his wife were frequent visitors at his house. There they became acquainted with his ward, Miss M'Auley. Her agreeable manners and excellent disposition soon made her a great favourite with them. They had no children themselves, and were, therefore, the more disposed to admire the good qualities, both of mind and heart, which they discovered in her. From their habits of familiar intercourse they became, each day, more and more attached to her; until at length, instead of meeting occasionally, they desired to have her entirely with themselves, and determined to adopt her as a daughter. The advantages of such a proposal were too obvious to be rejected; and, at their repeated solicitations, she removed to the beautiful country residence which they possessed near Dublin. Neither of the parties had any cause to regret the consequences of this arrangement. They were all that the fondest parents could be to her, and her grateful and devoted attachment caused them to forget that she was only their adopted child. But neither the advantages of her new position, nor the comforts she enjoyed, nor the attentions of her sincere and anxious friends, could relieve the anxiety or quiet the troubles of her mind on the great subject of religion. She still continued determined in her intention of professing herself a Catholic, and longed anxiously for an opportunity of communicating with some clergyman of that persuasion.

Notwithstanding all her private examination, and though she had no doubt as to the truth of Catholicity, there were yet several matters which could only be satisfactorily explained by an oral communication. Those who have been trained up from infancy in the habitual and frequent performance of religious duty, and whose minds, by a special favour from God, not often valued as it ought, have, from their first dawning, been directed and developed by religious teaching, may, perhaps, to some extent, but never adequately, conceive the agony by which the sincerely disposed and religious are tortured in such an important and trying position, as Miss M'Auley was now placed in;

where they are about to take a step, on which their interests
for eternity depend, where their past opinions, habits, feelings,
prejudices are undergoing an utter change—where the old man
is to be put off, and the new put on—where the very moral
and intellectual nature is being subjected to a complete and
fearful revolution, and where, moreover, the torture of that inward trial is aggravated by difficulties that often accompany it:
such are the fear of giving offence to valued friends, the separa-
ting from long-cherished connexions, the probability of being
exposed to obloquy, censure, and ridicule, the imputation of
bad motives from those whose good opinion it had ever been an
object to secure.   This forms an ordeal, which every reflecting
mind, that is under the influence of sincere and deliberate conviction, must be more or less prepared for, but by which, to
use a scriptural illustration, the wood, hay, and stubble of error
and corruption are to be purged away, and the soul purified as
by a fire.   Much, though not all, of this Miss M'Auley should
feel.   Her kind friends were unaware of her secret partiality for
the Catholic religion, and she, from a feeling which will be
easily understood, had a difficulty in making her wishes known
to them; yet, without doing so, it was morally impossible to
effect the object she had at heart, as her residence was some
miles from the city, and her kind friends would scarcely (so
strong was their attachment) permit her to be absent for one
instant without their knowing. where she went, and in what
she was occupied.

At length, one day, she alleged a reason for going alone to
Dublin.   She went into a milliner's shop, and having bought
some trifling articles of dress, she desired her servants to wait
with the carriage at that place until she should return.   It was
not far from the Roman Catholic chapel.

Almost breathless with haste, and trembling from the excitement of her feelings, she knocked at the residence of the clergymen, and inquired whether any of them were at home.   The
answer was in the affirmative, and she was introduced to the

presence of the Rev. Dr. Betagh. No one could be better suited to the occasion, or make a more favourable impression.

When the agitation of her excited feelings permitted her to explain the object of her visit, and the peculiar circumstances in which she was placed, he gave her such instruction and advice as she needed, removed the remaining difficulties she had, and appointed a day on which she was, if possible, to return again, and commence her preparation for the sacraments. Many were the difficulties she had to encounter in accomplishing that purpose—difficulties which, as the issue proved, might have been avoided by promptly and openly avowing her intentions. But she wished to put off a disclosure which, she feared, would prove so painful to her kind friends, until the very last moment; and it was not until she had made her first Communion that they became acquainted with the step she had taken. It is natural to suppose that they would have preferred her continuing of the same religious persuasion with themselves; but as her convictions were different, and her conscience directed otherwise, they heard her explanation with the most indulgent kindness, and said they would willingly allow her the same freedom of choice in the matter of religion, which, in similar circumstances, they would have desired themselves. She continued, therefore, to go to Mass, and they to church, without any diminution of their mutual esteem and affection.

When thus at liberty, she soon proved, by her regularity and piety, the strength of her religious convictions. She was most diligent in her observance of all the duties which religion required, and indefatigable in relieving the wants and sufferings of the poor. She had, indeed, little of her own, beyond a kind word of advice, or an affectionate expression of sympathy, to give; but she was often the ready and willing instrument of the bounty of others. Her adopted parents were good and charitable people, and Miss M'Auley was, on almost every occasion, the agent of their benevolence. But she did not confine herself to the relief of the corporal necessities of the

poor; she took pity on their spiritual destitution also, and, re-
membering the example of her father's usefulness, she resolved
to prove herself in all things worthy of his goodness. She collected the poor children of the neighbourhood in the Lodge,
which was kindly placed at her disposal for that purpose, and
devoted to their instruction all the leisure moments she could
spare. Her solicitude for the interests of the poor soon drew
around her many who hoped to find relief and consolation in
her advice, and who were not disappointed.

Everyone who had distress to be relieved, or affliction to be
mitigated, or troubles to be encountered, came to her, and she
gave consolation to the utmost of her ability. She soon became
a kind of missionary in the district. Her generous solicitude
was, on one occasion, exerted in behalf of a poor girl whose virtue
was exposed to the most imminent danger. She was a lady's
maid in a respectable family in the village. She had been
always remarkable for her piety and regularity, and possessed
an excellent character for propriety and good conduct. But,
unfortunately for herself, nature had given her more than an
ordinary share of personal attractions. A young man, the son
of the gentleman with whose family she was living, availed himself of the opportunity which was thus afforded him, and sought
to destroy her innocence. She was friendless and unprotected,
but she was, till then, innocent and faithful to her duty. She
rejected the proposals of the tempter; but his purpose was not
to be so easily baffled, and what he failed to effect by a direct
proposal, he sought insidiously to accomplish, by veiling his intentions under the mask of a pretended promise of marriage.

The poor girl, mistrusting his intention, and sensible of her
danger, sought the advice of Miss M'Auley, and requested her
assistance in escaping the ruin that threatened her. The advice she got—and it was the one that suited her case—was to
resign her situation immediately, and thus, as she was bound
to do, withdraw herself from the danger at once and without
delay.

Miss M'Auley engaged to pay her expenses until another situation should be procured. But profligacy was not so easily defeated in its designs. The young man heard and knew of her intention, and declared, with an oath, that if she removed from his father's house, he would spare no pains, and be deterred by no consideration of honour or delicacy, in his efforts to take away her character; and, therefore, that she would only be fleeing from a probable danger, to involve herself in another more terrible and certain. When the knowledge of this horrible determination was communicated by the unfortunate girl to her good friend, the feelings of the latter may be imagined, but cannot be described. The tempter seemed to have woven his web of perfidy with such unscrupulous art and perseverance, that escape seemed almost impossible. The only resource that presented itself was to procure for the object of her solicitude admission into one of those houses of refuge that were established in Dublin for females of her description.

She wrote without delay to the one that seemed to present the greatest probability of success, stated the urgency of the case, and the necessity for immediate admission. But no answer was received. A second application was made, but this also remained unanswered. Unable to account for the silence, and resolved to remain no longer in suspense, she went to seek, in person, the object which she had in vain solicited by letter. On applying at the House of Refuge, she discovered that though the management of the establishment and the care of the inmates was entrusted to the good religious, to whom the application was directed, they had nothing whatever to do with the admission of applicants. This was regulated by a committee of secular ladies, who met once a fortnight to consider the respective claims, and decide on the admission of the applicants; and it was in order to lay her case before this meeting that the answer of Miss M'Auley's application was delayed. She had to wait till then; and on the appointed day she presented herself before the committee, and urged the pressing nature of her case with all the earnestness and feeling in her power. She thought that a claim like that which she brought before their notice, would scarcely admit of deliberation, much less rejection; and great was her disappointment on finding that the committee had already decided on the persons to be admitted, and had no room for any others. In vain she represented to them the danger of delay, the consequences of refusal, and the almost inevitable ruin it would entail on the poor creature who had been for weeks looking forward, in all the anxiousness of hope, to such a protection against ruin that seemed otherwise inevitable.

The conditions which were absolutely necessary for admission could not be complied with either by Miss M'Auley or her poor client, and her application was in consequence rejected.

But the favourable moment was lost! The poor girl, disheartened at her want of success, and fancying, perhaps, in the hour of her despondency, that she had no way of escaping from the perils that surrounded her, was become a more easy prey to seduction. The result may be easily guessed, and was one other melancholy instance of innocence destroyed and profligacy triumphant. It will be seen hereafter that the lesson, however melancholy, which was afforded by this incident, was not lost upon Miss M'Auley; and that in the religious order which Providence made her the instrument of instituting, she took the most effectual precautions against the possibility of such a calamity. God may, in His far-seeing wisdom, have permitted one individual to fall, that thousands in after times may be saved from impending destruction.

To these works of charity, limited and unobtrusive as they were, she continued to devote much of her time; but after a few years, her kind friend, Mrs. Callaghan, was taken ill, and confined to her apartment. From this illness she never recovered. It was a lingering and tedious illness; and though not attended with any very violent pain, was sufficient, for the most part, to confine her to bed. This sickness was a new source of affliction to Miss M'Auley, and a new occasion of merit also. For many a long month did she watch by that bed, and prove the sincerity of her attachment by the most assiduous care. Everything which the most filial love could suggest to alleviate suffering or assuage pain, was done. The dear adopted child was ever near the bed to smooth the pillow on which her restless and wasted head reclined, or to soothe her weary limbs in the fitful movements of infirmity. She often read some book of moral and religious instruction—though this was a matter of no little inconvenience, as the only light which the tender eyes of the invalid could bear in the apartment was a shaded lamp placed upon the floor. For many weeks the only sleep she had was on a couch in the sick room, during the patient's intervals of repose; yet even then her mind was engaged in dreamy visions of charity and mercy to the poor. At one moment her imagination conjured up a group of poor orphan children, to whose wants she was ministering, arraying in new dresses their little limbs, or supplying their famishing lips with food; at another, it was a band of destitute outcast females—some abandoned by their parents, some deserted by their friends, some deprived of their natural protectors, some flying with horror from the proposals of libertine seducers—that would present themselves to her excited fancy. Then the scene would suddenly change, and the picture would consist of bands of young women engaged in the various occupations of household industry; and so the mind would be occupied, until alarmed and overpowered by the wild revellings of her imagination, she often started from the broken slumbers, and burst into tears. "Catherine," the sick woman would sometimes say to her, "I almost wish you never went to sleep, you frighten me so much, and seem to suffer so much trouble in your moments of repose."

Was it that her zeal, bursting beyond the ordinary course of usefulness to which it was confined, loved to embody itself in these visions of benevolence to her kind? Or, could it have been that God manifested to her, as to many of His sainted children of yore, the exalted mission of usefulness and mercy to

which, a few years later, she was to be called? But the solicitude of Miss M'Auley was not confined to the bodily infirmities
or pains of her dear and valued friend. She wished to make
her a partaker of the religious advantages which she herself
enjoyed; and the great object for which she prayed with many
sighs and tears was, that the sick patient hould receive the
grace of conversion, and be reconciled to the Church before she
died. She had endeavoured to prepare her for this, in some
measure, by speaking, from time to time, on religious subjects,
and by explaining to her the nature of Catholic truths and practices; and, availing herself, at length, of a favourable opportunity
that presented itself, she earnestly recommended its adoption.
But there were many difficulties in the way. The lady herself
had no objection, she said, to die a member of the Catholic
communion, but such a step would afflict her husband beyond
expression. He had always been kind and attentive, and proved
himself on every occasion a most affectionate and devoted partner; and how could she thus requite him for all his kindness?
They had always lived in peace and harmony together! How
could she, by embracing another creed, sever, as it were, the
bonds that united them together, and embitter his declining years?
There was, she said, another reason that influenced her even
more than these, and rendered it impossible to comply with her
request. This reason she was unwilling to disclose. Her kind
attendant was pressing in her entreaty, and, at length, she said:
"I think my husband would be so dissatisfied and displeased
with your interference, that he would be very likely to deprive
you for ever of any portion of his property; and I cannot consent to any measure that would prove so disastrous to you."
Surprised at such a proof of her generous affection, and determined that, in an affair of such consequence, she should not be
influenced by this consideration, she continued to urge her
proposal, entreated her to lay aside such apprehensions, and
assured her, that the poorest habitation and the humblest position in life, would be a thousand times more acceptable than the

wealth of the universe, if it were to be purchased at such a price, and secured by the loss of one so valued and esteemed. She would be content, she said, to live in the humblest cottage for the remainder of her days, if she could only see her benefactress a Catholic before she died. Such a proof of disinterested affection and self-sacrificing love was not to be resisted; and she, at length, consented, provided arrangements could be made to effect it without the knowledge of her husband; and added, " Surely the faith which leads you to work by charity, must be holy and sent by God. You have, with saintly sweetness, borne with all my peevishness and impatience; and I rejoice to embrace the religion which has sanctified you." Delighted at her success, she lost no time in availing herself of the permission that was thus given her; and Mr. Callaghan's absence on business having afforded a convenient opportunity, she applied to a clergyman who was then residing in the vicinity of her residence. He received her into the Church. The hours of the good lady were already numbered; and before he could repeat his visit, she was no more. She died in the arms of her kind and devoted friend, who had at last the happiness of seeing her most anxious hope fulfilled, by the conversion of one she had loved so well.

The goodness and generosity of the deceased lady may be inferred from what has been stated in the preceding pages. The following incident will serve to show it in a still stronger light:—

Her husband having been the maker of his own fortune, had a number of relatives not as well off in the world as himself, and who, therefore, hoped to come in for a share of his wealth, as he had no family of his own. It was a source of great annoyance and jealousy to them that Miss M'Auley occupied the place, which they thought they should have occupied themselves. They envied the happiness and good fortune she obtained. They attributed it all to the partiality which Mrs. Callaghan entertained for her, and resolved to wreak their vengeance on her. In the furtherance of this intention, they endeavoured to sow disunion between her and her husband. They sent her anonymous letters, full of the most insulting allusions to her domestic afflictions, and most outraging to her feelings. She knew the handwriting, and was thus able to trace them to a young man who was a connexion of the family. Some short time after, the mother of this young man called on her to solicit her interference with Mr. C. on his behalf. She went down stairs to see her, and having heard the nature of the application, she returned to Miss M'Auley, with whom she had been conversing. " Mrs. ——," said she, " has been talking to me about her son. He has been offered, it seems, a commission in the army, provided he can pay down immediately £300. Such an opportunity may never present itself again, and she wishes me to induce my husband to give the money." " Well," replied Miss M'Auley, " and will you not do so?" " Can I," exclaimed she, " exert myself in favour of a man who has in so malicious a manner endeavoured to deprive me of the affection of my husband; who has tried, without any provocation, to wound my feelings, and insult me?" She opened a drawer, which contained the letters she had received, and, taking them out, said: " Were I now to read these, I could not be prevailed on by any solicitation to serve him; but I will act nobly and generously towards him;" and taking them in her hand, she threw them into the fire. She then went to her husband, stated the object of her request, and got the money.

After her death, matters went on in the family as usual, Mr. Callaghan attending to his professional engagements, and Miss M'Auley to the works of charity, which she had again resumed. But, after some time, advancing years brought with them to Mr. Callaghan increasing infirmities, which became aggravated, perhaps, by his late domestic affliction.

If the most devoted tenderness and the most untiring solicitude could arrest the progress of age and illness, he would have long continued a healthy man, for his affectionate ward did all that a daughter could do to comfort his declining years; but though they may delay or lighten the progress of infirmity, no solicitude, however diligent, and no care, however devoted, can arrest it altogether; and the health of her dear friend began visibly to decline. After a little .time he was confined entirely to his chamber, or, at least, his house. One evening, as they were conversing together, he abruptly said to her: " Catherine, what shall I leave you at my death? Will you be satisfied with a thousand pounds?" Annoyed and disturbed at the question, she expressed her grief at being addressed on such a subject, and assured him that the matter had never occupied her thoughts. " She did not want money," she said, " and would not know what to do with a thousand pounds." " You would not know," observed he, falling back in his chair, laughing, " what to do with a thousand pounds. Well, I know what you would do with it. You would do a great deal of good with it, at all events." Each day he became weaker and more infirm, and soon began to exhibit symptoms that his life was drawing to a close. His ward, who had his spiritual, yet more than his temporal, interests at heart, became filled with the most serious and anxious apprehensions, and prayed earnestly that, before his death, he might be reconciled to the Church by a sincere conversion. He was a good and kind-hearted man, blameless in all the relations of life, and generous in his charities to the poor; but she desired that he should add the treasure of the true faith to the number of his other virtues, and secure for himself the possession of the one thing, that, of all others, was the most necessary. He now devoted somewhat of his attention to the subject of religious controversy, read many religious works, and was most liberal and unprejudiced in his opinions. She was, moreover, dearer to him, and enjoyed his confidence and regard to a greater extent than any other person; yet she felt the utmost difficulty in addressing him on such a topic, however great its importance may be, and could only pray fervently and earnestly that, out of His great mercy, God would confer this favour upon her and him. At length he began to sink rapidly, and, as she was determined to leave nothing undone on her part to secure his conversion, she waited on the attending physician, and begged to know for what length of time did he think his life was likely to be prolonged. " That is quite uncertain," said he; " the nature of his illness is such, that he may live for a month, or he may die to-morrow !" Alarmed at the urgency of the occasion, she knew not what to do. The Rev. Mr. Armstrong was her friend and spiritual adviser, since the elevation of Dr. Murray to the episcopacy. She had recourse to him for counsel, and told him what she had just heard from the physician. He advised her to lose not a day in speaking to her benefactor upon the subject, and promised to remember and pray for a blessing upon her efforts in his customary ministration at the altar. The very next morning she resolved to introduce the topic of religion, and recommend it to his acceptance. But when the moment came for doing so, her courage failed her, and she had not strength to do it. She made several attempts, but could not give utterance to a word. At length she made up her mind to make the attempt, no matter what the consequence might be. She came to his bedside, but even then, unable to give expression to her feelings, sank down upon her knees, clasped his hand in her's, and, overpowered by emotion, burst into an agony of tears. The sick man was frightened, and thought that some dreadful calamity had happened. He asked her, again and again, what was the matter, and did all in his power to calm her agitation. When he had, in some degree, succeeded, she told him that the cause of her agitation was a matter concerning which she was most anxious, but yet afraid to speak to him. Not being able to conceive what this matter might be, and feeling hurt at the idea that there should be any subject on which she was afraid to speak to him, he asked whether he had refused her anything she had ever asked of him, or had ever given her any reason to doubt the sincerity of his affection. " No, no," said she, " it is not for myself, it is on your account that I am uneasy." A thought flashed across his mind. " Is it," said he,

" that you think me in imminent danger?" " I do, indeed, think you are in danger," replied she, " and know that you are very bad; but it is not the state of your health that troubles me so much, it is the danger of your immortal soul, which I believe to be endangered by your dying in any other than the ' Church of Rome,' and without the aid of those spiritual advantages which Christ has appointed for persons in your condition. The very thought of such a calamity is to me most painful and heartrending."

" Dear Catherine," her kind friend replied, " be tranquil. You have exerted yourself on my account most unnecessarily. I have a firm confidence in God, and reliance on his mercy! I have read a great deal on religious matters, and have, I trust, acted uprightly, in following, according to my conscience, the religion which I profess."

Seeing that she was far, very far, from being satisfied with this answer, he told her to be calm for the present, and promised to speak to her some other time upon the subject.

She requested him not to postpone the consideration of the subject longer than the following day; and on the following morning he was himself the first to resume the conversation.

" Well," said he, " am I to introduce this very exciting subject again? I must do so to gratify you. You wish me, I suppose, to become a Roman Catholic, whether I am convinced or not?"

After some further conversation, she asked him whether he would read some good and approved work on the differences between their respective Churches; and, on his remarking that the state of his health did not then permit him to do so, she requested that he would, at least, permit her to introduce her friend, the Rev. Mr. Armstrong, to have some further conversation on the subjects that were at issue between them.

" As you desire it," he said. " I have no objection; and if he can succeed in proving the faith of Catholics to be better and holier than that of which I am a member, I promise to embrace it upon the instant."

She lost no time in availing herself of the permission he had given, went to the reverend gentleman, and introduced him to her friend. The sick man received him, and listened to his explanations of doctrinal subjects with marked and anxious attention. At his rising to depart, he begged, of his own accord, that he would be good enough to renew his visit at his earliest convenience. What was at first mere courtesy, soon ripened into a feeling of the deepest interest, and his mind began to open by degrees to the reception of the truth. Difficulties that he thought insuperable ceased to be such when presented to him in a different light from that in which he had been accustomed to consider them; and the conviction was at last brought home to his mind that the true Church of Christ was that which, owing to his own mistaken opinions and the involuntary prejudices of his early education, he had always looked on as apostate. He had no motive to do violence to his convictions, no motives of self-interest to dispute the supremacy of his conscience, no link to bind him to error other than the prejudice in which he had been educated; and when that link was broken, its hold upon his mind was gone for ever. He avowed his intention of becoming a Catholic, and sought immediate admission inside the pale of that Church, from which the circumstances of his birth and his position in society, and not any insensibility or obduracy of his own, had hitherto excluded him.

Who can tell what must have been the feelings of Miss M'Auley, when her prayers, her solicitude, her untiring exertions in his behalf were at length crowned with success? She saw him admitted into the Church, and to the participation of the sacraments, which he received with sentiments of the most sincere and heartfelt devotion.

He survived his conversion but a short time, during which his piety was most exemplary.

It may be supposed that the generous self-devotion and assiduity of his adopted daughter was not diminished by a circumstance which endeared him to her still more.

When he died, it was found that he had bequeathed to her all his property, which was very considerable.

What she did with his property, and what she did with herself, the reader will find explained to him in the following account of the Sisters of Mercy.

A young lady who comes into possession of a considerable fortune, will be likely to have suitors; and if she remain unmarried, it will not be for want of persons to solicit the honour of her hand.

Miss M'Auley, in a short time after the death of her good friend, was honoured with the attentions of more than one individual, that would have scarcely condescended to notice a poor orphan girl, merely dependant on the bounty of her friends. But money makes great changes in the opinions of men like these; and many, who, before, passed her by unnoticed, now sought with the most eager anxiety the honour of a matrimonial alliance. Some had recourse to the kind offices of her friends to urge their suit, and advocate their cause; but it was all in vain. She rejected at once, and indiscriminately, their addresses, and declared to all those whom it might concern, that her firm determination was to lead a single life, and to renounce for ever any intentions of marriage. Nor was this avowal at all displeasing to her own immediate friends, inasmuch as it seemed to secure to them the reversion of the property and fortune after her death, and perhaps, also, the partial enjoyment of it during her life. With such hopes and advantages in prospective, it may be supposed that they were not overanxious to advocate the suits of those who aspired to the honour of her hand. What her final intentions were she made known to the Rev. Mr. Armstrong alone. He was aware of every circumstance of her life since she had become a practical Catholic; and he knew also the events of the last few years, by which Providence seemed to be, as it were, preparing her for some special destiny, which she was to fulfil. To him alone she communicated the intention she had formed of devoting her means to the relief of the sick and destitute, and of establishing some

I

permanent institution for the mitigation of their many sufferings. This was a project she had been long contemplating. It was ever present to her mind, even when she was a mere dependant upon the bounty of others, and looked forward to it even when there seemed no human probability of her ever being able to carry it into effect. Now that God gave her the means of doing so, she resolved on commencing the good work without delay. The reverend friend just mentioned was the only one that was yet aware of what she intended to do. At his suggestion, it was resolved to commence an establishment immediately, and in some public and respectable quarter of the city. " It had been too much the custom," he said, " for Catholics to have their charitable institutions in the bye-places of the capital, in some obscure street or lane, that often was almost inaccessible. It was desirable to make a change in this respect, and that Catholics should bring their charitable institutions more prominently before the world. Thus, their light would not be under a bushel, but so placed that all might see and admire, and be edified at the good works they witnessed; nor was it right that, in this respect, they should be placed at a disadvantage when compared with their Protestant fellow-citizens." It was not considered advisable to take a house, built already for other purposes, and which they should have some difficulty in adapting to their use, but a plot of ground, that never had been built upon, and erect, for the honour and glory of God, an edifice that had never been devoted to the pleasures or the follies of fashionable life, or, perhaps, sullied by insults to their religion, and which should be holy in its first application as in its subsequent use, and be consecrated to Him from its very foundations. In accordance with this suggestion, a piece of ground was purchased in Baggot-street, a healthy and respectable part of the city. She got a plan and estimate, from a competent person, of a building that would answer all her intended purposes, and gave directions to have it commenced immediately.

A severe family affliction befell her about this time. Her

sister had been long labouring under some indisposition, which had gradually undermined her constitution, and, at length, developed itself in a disease of a most incurable character. The invalid claimed and obtained from her sister the most unwearied attention. Nothing could be more devoted than her kind care and affection; but finding it impossible to attend to her patient as she wished to do, and, at the same time, to superintend her new building in Baggot-street, and also keep up her establishment in the country, she resolved on giving up the latter. The house and demesne were accordingly sold, the servants dismissed, and, having thus become more at liberty, she took up her abode with her brother-in-law. Thus she was able to watch at the sick bed of her dying sister, and, without much inconvenience, pay a visit every day to the new building that was in progress of erection.

After her sister's death, whom she had the happiness to see reconciled to the Church in her last moments, Miss M'Auley continued to devote herself to the care and superintendence of her children. She had promised their dying parent that she would be a mother to them; and such she proved herself in deed, providing for their wants, and devising means for their improvement, with a solicitude as anxious and devoted as any mother could do. With all these duties and anxieties, however, she did not lose sight of the great work she had on hands, and visited the establishment in Baggot-street almost every day, expecting much and earnestly its final completion. The new building had already made considerable progress; and the people in the neighbourhood, and the persons who were passing by, often asked each other, for what the " large house" was intended, but no one yet could tell. The labourers, who were employed upon it, could not tell; nor the tradesmen, not even the contractor or the architect. They knew it was being erected at the expense of a Miss M'Auley; and some were charitable enough to say, that having lately come into the possession of a great deal of money, she did not seem to know very well what to do with it. Her relatives, too, would come frequently to see what was doing in Baggot-street, look about attentively, and make inquiries like any of the others—for as little as any of the others, did they know what she meant to do. There could be no doubt, they would say, but that it was a useless and wasteful expenditure of money; but none of them ventured to ask a word of explanation.

In the summer of the year 1827, the new building in Baggot-street was completed, and ready for the purposes to which it was to be applied. The first and principal one which Miss M'Auley had then in view, was the instruction of the poor; and to prepare herself for the most efficient accomplishment thereof, she resolved on becoming acquainted with the system of instruction that was adopted in the most approved and best-regulated schools. The Kildare-street Society was then in extensive operation; and whatever its other faults may have been—and they were many and considerable—there can be no doubt that the system of instruction pursued by it was a great improvement on that which had been previously employed. Better, indeed, have since been devised and carried into practical operation in the schools of the National Board of Education, but it was, when first introduced, the very best of its time. To acquire such a practical knowledge of its working as might be rendered available for her own objects, Miss M'Auley made several visits to the schools that had been established by the Kildare-street Board; but while she admired the practical utility and great efficiency of its educational system, she also was sorry to find that many Catholic children, attracted by the worldly advantages it held out, were brought within the sphere of its peculiar religious influence, and while imbibing earthly knowledge, were also forced to imbibe the poison of error that was insidiously infused into the draught. Though a Catholic, and in that respect looked on, perhaps, with no very favourable eye by the managers, she was also connected with a respectable Protestant family, and occupied a respectable position in the world, and, therefore, received some degree of attention. She made frequent and protracted visits, and, while she inspected the progress of the pupils, and saw how knowledge was communicated, her jealous and attentive eye noted the several Catholic children that were present, and learned from them the names, residences, and occupations of their parents. At a subsequent period, when her schools were opened, she prevailed on the latter to withdraw their children from the danger of seduction, and place them under her own care. The schools were soon opened. The poor children in the neighbourhood were invited to attend, and came in considerable numbers. A few kind and charitable ladies volunteered their services, and the new establishment commenced its career of usefulness with every prospect of success.

Hitherto, as has been already stated, Miss M'Auley had resided with her friends, but the new building being prepared for her reception, she began to take up her abode in it occasionally, according as the nature of her duties required. She gave admittance also to a few respectable young women, to whom such accommodation was necessary, until suitable situations could be prepared for them. Several of those ladies who had consented to give her the aid of their services in the school, seeing the good she did, expressed a willingness, with the consent of their friends, of devoting themselves more fully to the promotion of the objects she had in view. Her niece, too, though not yet a Catholic, took a deep interest in the various objects of charity, and worked as zealously and devotedly as any of the others. To draw down the divine blessing on the undertaking, it was resolved to place the whole establishment under the divine protection, and measures were taken to have this done with all the necessary solemnity. Its foundress had a peculiar devotion to the festival of Our Blessed Lady of Mercy. The 24th of September, on which that festival is celebrated, was approaching, and she wrote to his Grace the Most Rev. Dr. Murray, for permission to have her little chapel blessed and consecrated on that day, and thereby to have a religious character, as well as the necessary religious

I 2

sanction, given to the work to which she was so ardently devoted. This prelate, who had been from the very beginning
her sincere friend, and who was ever ready to encourage and
sanction any work by which the glory of God may be effectually
promoted, consented without hesitation; and on the appointed
morning the little chapel was solemnly blessed, and the entire
establishment placed under the invocation of Our Blessed Lady
of Mercy. This, from being the title of one solitary house, was
destined, in the designs of God's wisdom, to become the title
and distinctive appellation of a numerous and widely-extended
order.

The works that God has specially favoured, and which He has
destined to be the means of great and enduring good, have
almost always been humble and unpretending in the beginning.
They have also been very often exposed to trial and opposition.
It was thus with His Church; it was thus with the religious institutions of many an age; and thus, also, it was to be with the
House of Our Lady of Mercy.

On the very morning of its institution, while yet its little
chapel rang with the voice of prayer, and was filled with the
sweet odour of the incense, which—fittest emblem of prayer—
had ascended from ministering hands to greet the Saviour's
presence upon the altar, some were found to speak doubtingly,
if not harshly, of the character of the establishment in which
they were assembled. The motives and the wisdom of its
foundress were, in her very hearing, canvassed; and even mur-
murs of censure and disapproval reached her ears. In charity
we are bound to think, that those who thus expressed themselves,
thought they were doing well in censuring and condemning an
undertaking which they—short-sighted men—deemed dangerous
or unsafe, as it was then presented to them; but it was a poor
recompense for all her generous and devoted zeal, and all her
noble and disinterested sacrifices, not to have waited, at least,
until it was seen what character it would assume. Painful it
must have been to her to hear a disapproval from any one, much

more from those whose zeal for the divine glory, and charity for the suffering poor, should have been even greater than her own. Nor was this opposition confined to the occasion of this first ceremony; it continued for several years to thwart and impede, as far as it could, the progress of the institute. But God watched over that institute as His own work, brought it to a prosperous issue, and took care that the opposition should be eventually unsuccessful.

It was with reference to this opposition, so prematurely and injudiciously made to the establishment of the order of the Sisters of Mercy, that a distinguished prelate of the Irish Church made use of the following words:—

" I look on Mrs. M'Auley as one selected by heaven to be specially endowed with benediction. Her heart is overflowing with the charity of the Redeemer, whose all-consuming love burns within her breast. No female has ever done more for sorrowing, suffering humanity than she has done. She may well rejoice over those whom she has been instrumental in snatching from the enemy's grasp, and confidently claim a blessing from heaven on her future exertions. I would venture to say, that her name is written in the Book of Life; and I feel convinced that any individual or society, presuming by word or deed to injure her institute, will draw down upon themselves the lash, the scourge of the Almighty, even in this world."

The only effect which this opposition produced upon her mind, was to make her examine more thoroughly and profoundly the motives which influenced her conduct. She tried to discover whether it might not be governed by some principle which religion would not sanction, and began to fear lest her zeal, however well meant, was not approved by God.

She resolved, therefore, to seek advice from her ecclesiastical superiors, and to be guided by them in her difficulty. His Grace the Most Rev. Dr. Murray had been from the beginning her sincerest friend. He was also the person to whom religion bade her have recourse, and whose authority was to be, in her

regard, even as the authority of God. If he approved and
sanctioned her undertaking, it mattered little what others said
or did.   If he objected to her establishment, it would be a sign
that her views and undertaking had not been dictated by the
Spirit of God.   She sought an interview accordingly, and laid
before   him   the   nature   of   her   benevolent foundation, the
objects she sought to accomplish, and the methods by which
these objects were to be attained.   Fame, or distinction, or men's
praises, she sought not.   She wished not to interfere with such
others as might be labouring in the same field.   She offered to
resign into his hands the house she had just completed, for
any purposes of religion he might wish, and asked for herself
but the poorest apartment in the house, and the merit of labouring in any capacity, however humble, to carry out his charitable
intentions.   No one could better appreciate the generosity
of such an offer than the prelate to whom it was made.   He
had been, from her very conversion, the witness of her zeal
and piety.   He knew her worth, and had no difficulty in perceiving that her conduct throughout had been entirely influenced
by the purest and the most devout charity.   To her proposal of
committing the establishment to the care of some one of the
religious institutions then in Dublin, he answered in the most
decided negative.   He felt that the same benevolent and generous spirit to which it was indebted for its existence, would best
preside over its subsequent exertions, and conduct it to eventual
success.   Every good work, he said, was ever destined to be
opposed and contradicted, and for trials she should be prepared.
In accordance with these views, he gave his most earnest and
distinct approval to her undertaking, and took preliminary steps
to place it on a footing of efficient and permanent stability.   He
permitted the inmates to assume an uniform religious dress, and
visit the hospitals and private houses, whenever the sick and
poor required religious instruction and consolation.

It was not the custom, at this period, for the members of the
various religious societies and congregations in Dublin, to visit

the public hospitals, as they have for some years been in the habit of doing. The Catholic patients who were ill, and wished for the ministry of a clergyman of their persuasion, were, indeed, permitted to avail themselves thereof without impediment; but they were not visited by any of those good and charitable religious women, that may be at this day seen in most of the hospitals, going round from one sick bed to another, and inspiring their poor occupants with sentiments of hope and resignation. Miss M'Auley wished to remedy this evil; and knowing that the greater number of the patients that were received into these hospitals were Roman Catholics, she resolved on obtaining access to them, for the purpose of communicating to them religious instruction and consolation. In the furtherance of this object, she paid a visit one day, accompanied by a few of her associates, to Sir Patrick Dun's Hospital, of which her friend, Dr. C., was head physician. He and one or two of the governors accompanied her through the wards, and showed her the several objects of curiosity that are usually shown to visitors that take an interest in the means which modern science and philanthropy have employed for the mitigation of human suffering.

While her young friends were dispersed throughout the wards, Miss M'Auley remained in conversation with the doctor and the gentlemen who accompanied her; and, in the course of conversation, took an opportunity of asking, whether there would be any objection, on the part of the managers, to her visiting the hospital from time to time, for the purpose of imparting religious consolation to the poor suffering inmates. They answered that not the smallest obstacle would be thrown in her way, and that they were perfectly at liberty, and perfectly welcome, to visit the patients whensoever and as often as they pleased. She availed herself without delay of the permission that was thus given her; and since then religious instruction and consolation have been regularly given in this hospital, where, until then, no visits exclusively religious were allowed to be made, except those of the clergymen who were called in to administer the last rites of their Church to the dying patients that required their aid.

In her efforts to procure the right of access to this and to the other institutions, in which she was equally successful, she availed herself of the influence which her position in the world gave her. She knew that persons would more willingly accede to the request of one who occupied a distinguished or prominent position in society, than to that made by individuals of humbler rank. Whenever, therefore, she wished to urge her application for admittance into any of these establishments, where she thought her services were likely to be useful, she always took care to pay her first visit in her own carriage, and attended by her own servants. She did this, not from any motive of ostentation or display, but from the wish to remove the obstacles that the world might raise to the fulfilment of her charitable designs. She wished to vanquish the world and its prejudices by its own weapons. Having done so, she had attained her object, and, in the course of a few months, she disposed of her equipage, gave the price of it to the poor, and never resumed it again.

About this time she was visited by a severe and, to her, trying calamity, by the death of her esteemed friend, the Rev. Mr. Armstrong. It has been already stated, that from the very beginning he had been her adviser in all the things relating to the foundation of her establishment, and had taken the warmest interest in its progress. When others blamed, or criticised, or censured, he was always ready to comfort and sympathise with her in all the contradictions to which she was exposed; and it was afflicting now to lose him, when his advice and sympathy were needed as much as ever.

On his deathbed he requested an interview with his Grace the Most Rev. Dr. Murray; and when the Archbishop entered his apartment, said, that the reason which made him seek the favour then conferred upon him, was his solicitude for Miss M'Auley, and her young establishment in Baggot-street. He knew her worth, he said, had watched over the progress of her undertaking, and saw that it was one that promised to be of great and signal utility to the Church, and particularly the poor. He was convinced that its foundress was raised up by Providence, as a special instrument of mercy to His suffering and afflicted children in this land; and from his dying bed he besought his Grace to watch over and protect it, and to extend to it and to its members the benefits of his patronage and support. It is scarcely necessary to add, from what has been already stated, that this appeal was most favourably received, and that the prelate realised, to the fullest extent, the confidence that was thus reposed in him.

· The poor schools attached to the house in Baggot-street were very extensive, and at this time were very well attended. The poor girls from all parts of the city were anxious to get admission, and it is unnecessary to say that admission was denied to none. It was deemed advisable also to establish a school for young females whose parents, though in comfortable circumstances, were not able to meet the expenses of a regular boarding-school education. Such pupils attended only during the day, and after the time which is usually devoted to instruction in day schools, returned to their homes in the afternoon. By this means, the blessings of a good religious education was communicated to a class of persons for whom, in most places, a very insufficient provision is made. In the visitation of the sick, also, Miss M'Auley and her companions often met with young children utterly destitute and helpless, many of them deprived of their parents at a very early age, and abandoned, in consequence, to all the horrors of poverty and ignorance, and very frequently to consequences of a yet more melancholy description.

Wishing to relieve, at least, some of the misery they witnessed, and with a vivid sense of the claim which the orphan has upon the Christian's charity, Miss M'Auley permitted her associates to take each an orphan child into the house, and instruct her, not only in her religious duties, but also in such other branches of knowledge and female industry as might enable them to provide for their subsistence in after life.

The applications for admission into the orphanage were in a short time more numerous than the managers, however well disposed, could possibly comply with.

Another and most interesting object of their solicitude, was the poor young woman who was deprived of the ordinary means of assistance and support, whether by the death of friends or by the want of employment. It is evident, that in a large city such females are inevitably exposed to great and imminent danger. What, for instance, can be more distressing and perilous, than the condition of a poor servant, who is compelled to leave her situation by ill-health or other cause, and who has no home or friend to give her shelter and protection, until she is fortunate enough to procure another? For a few weeks she may be able to support herself by the little saving she has been able to make out of her scanty wages; when this is gone, she must have recouse to the pawnbroker, because the hard necessity of providing the means of subsistence is sufficient to overcome, for the time, every minor consideration. However fond she may be of her articles of dress, and however necessary she may deem them to enable her to apply for a situation with any prospect of success, they disappear under the stern pressure of hunger, and one by one are pledged, or sold, to procure bread. When all are gone, and starvation stares her in the face, and the landlord is pressing for his arrears of rent, what is she to do? If nature has been liberal in its gifts, and favoured her with personal attractions, her position becomes one of the most serious danger, and in large cities has often been attended with the most calamitous results. To obviate some at least of these, and rescue some of the poor females from danger, Miss M'Auley fitted up a part of her house for their accommodation.

Besides those to whom she gave admission, she endeavoured to procure situations for several others; and thus was able to extend her charitable solicitude to a considerable number, who,

in addition to receiving from her the means of subsistence, received also religious instruction and advice, of which very
frequently they stood in need.

Of the good effected by Miss M'Auley in rescuing poor females
from danger, it may not be uninteresting to give one or two
instances.

She heard at one time of a young girl who had been induced,
after much solicitation, to leave her natural guardians, and place
herself under the protection of a certain gentleman, whose intentions were not of the most honourable character. Miss M'Auley,
then a Nun—for it occurred after her profession—accompanied
by a respectable Catholic clergyman, went to her lodgings
to make an effort to rescue her from impending ruin. It was
late at night, and the place of her abode was, after some delay
and difficulty, discovered. When Miss M'Auley and her reverend
friend arrived, the young lady and her companion were sitting
in the drawing-room. The clergyman was the first who entered,
and the instant that he presented himself, the wretched young
man, in a frenzy of rage, grasped a pistol that was near him, and
swore that, if he came a step farther, he would most assuredly
fire it at him. Miss M'Auley then presented herself, and the
young man, who had been acquainted with her previously, was
immediately struck with sentiments of shame and remorse·
"Miss M'Auley," said he, "I never felt humbled till this moment;"
and conscience-stricken and penitent, he permitted them to take
away the unresisting female, who was thus rescued from almost
inevitable destruction.

On another occasion, a young, and rather well-looking female
made application for admission to the house in Baggot-street. It
was at a late hour in the evening, and this circumstance, together
with a certain wildness of look and manner, gave rise to most
serious suspicions. She declared that she was the daughter of
a respectable gentleman, who resided in a town in the south of
Ireland; that family differences and troubles had driven her from
her father's house, and that she walked all the way to Dublin, in

K

the hope of getting into some house of refuge in the city. On her arrival, she made application to one, but alas! the good woman who answered her knock at the door, told her, that unfortunately there existed not the slightest chance of her being received. In vain did she declare that she knew no one in Dublin; that she had no home to go to; and no one to give her even a morsel of bread. In the anguish of her mind, and the utter hopelessness of her position, she asked at last whether, if she remained at the street door till morning there would be any chance of her being even then admitted? But there was still no hope held out to her; and as a last resource, perhaps, to get rid of her clamorous importunity, she was recommended to make application to the House of Mercy, in Baggot-street. Miss M'Auley heard her statement, and though not giving implicit credence to it all, she yet thought it would be prudent to give her shelter for the night. In the morning, while she was making further inquiries on the subject, one of the young ladies happened accidentally to see her, and recognised her immediately as one with whom she was previously acquainted. "The father of the young person," she said, "was an attorney, and had married a second time. The introduction of a step-mother was not very agreeable to the younger members of the family, more especially to the grown up daughters and in all probability, it was the dissension arising from this circumstance that had led to the rash step which this young female had taken." This proved to be the fact. After some time a situation was provided for her as governess in a respectable family.

If providence had not directed her steps to the kind and charitable ladies in Baggot-street, it requires no great sagacity to discover the fate that would, in all probability, have awaited her.

The establishment in Baggot-street, was making itself extensively useful. The ladies, who had the charge of it, not only attended the sick, and had a large school for the education of poor children, but they also had a small Orphanage, and a place of refuge for poor destitute females ; yet, notwithstanding this varied usefulness, it was in a somewhat anomalous position. A Catholic visitor, however highly he may value its services, or be edified by the piety of its members, would miss that peculiar religious form, which ought to distinguish similar communities, and that regular religious organisation, which should give both stability to its existence, and efficacy to its operations. It could be looked on, at best, but as a work of private charity, presided over by individual zeal, and dependent for its continuance on the mere will of her to whom it was indebted for its existence. It was, therefore, desirable that the Church should take it more formally under its protection than it had hitherto done, invest it with a more religious character, and give to it a more enduring existence than it would be likely to have, if solely dependent upon the good disposition of its foundress and her associates.

No one was more sensible of these defects than Miss M'Auley herself, and no one more ardently desired to have them remedied. She had repeatedly applied to his Grace the Archbishop of Dublin, to take her house and her associates under his immediate protection, and give to them whatever religious form and character he may deem desirable. It soon, indeed became absolutely necessary, that something should be done. Many, even well disposed Catholics, were beginning to take offence at the strange and unusual appearance which the establishment had assumed. It was neither a convent nor a private house; neither a religious community, nor yet a public establishment. Remonstrances were made to the foundress by friends, as well as by those who were not friendly: sometimes in the language of kind and well-meant expostulation, and not unfrequently in terms of unqualified disapproval. She often received, by post, letters, written and addressed in a very disrespectful manner. Several of these, though anonymous, she had no difficulty of tracing to their source; but matters had come to such a pitch, and Miss M'Auley's position was made so unpleasant, that something was at once to be done, to rescue her from the pain of such unmerited annoyance. For her own part, she could have borne it all in patience, and found strength and consolation in prayer to Him, who was himself insulted and reviled; and who has said to His followers, " Blessed are you when men shall revile you, and speak falsely against you in my name. Rejoice and be glad, for your reward is exceeding great in heaven." But she could not wish that those who were united to her in the sacred work of charity, should suffer also, nor that the institution, which she had laboured so long and axiously, and at such expense to perfect, should be injured in the public estimation, and be thereby obstructed in its career of usefulness. But God, who permitted her for a time to be thus tried, had chosen her for his own high purposes; and in trials and tribulations, wished that her virtue should be made perfect. In his own time, and when the fitting season came, he took care that these trials should cease, and the great object, for which she had longed and prayed, should be brought, at length, to a successful termination.

One day, when the horizon of her hopes was more than usually clouded, and her mind unusually depressed by the difficulties that encompassed her, his Grace the Archbishop sought an interview, and announced his determination to comply with her wishes respecting the future condition of the establishment, and invest it, without delay, with a solemn and religious character.

As the objects which the foundress sought to attain, namely, the spiritual and corporal works of mercy, were, in their full extent, the objects of no other religious institute, it was deemed advisable to have the new congregation perfectly unconnected with any other ; to have it regulated and governed by its own rules, and to have it also designated by a separate and distinctive appellation. No more appropriate title could be selected to express its purpose, and describe its character, than that which it then was determined to give it: " The Institute of our Blessed Lady of Mercy." An Order of Mercy had already existed in the Church; it was founded by St. Peter Nolasco, in the thirteenth century. Like that, which in after times received the same name, that Order was called into existence, by the spirit which prompted holy men to relieve the necessities, and mitigate the sufferings of their afflicted brethren. In the twelfth and thirteenth centuries, the Christians of the northern shores of the Mediterranean, were exposed to the predatory attacks of the Moors. The latter, from their superior skill in nautical affairs, and the number and strength of their ships, were able to bid defiance to any force that the Christian governments of Europe had power, at least singly, to bring against them. Their fleets rode triumphant on the waters and carried terror and dismay along the coasts of Spain and Italy. The inhabitants of Tunis and Algiers were moreover, accustomed to send out privateers to cruise along the coasts for the purposes of piracy and plunder. Sometimes they contented themselves with attacking such merchant vessels as they happened to fall in with; but not unfrequently they made sudden descents upon the countries that lay along the shore, and, after plundering the houses, carried away into captivity, the hapless natives that fell into their hands. The condition of these Christian slaves, in the homes of their Mahometan masters, was truly deplorable. The lot of the slave is a hard and wretched one, in even its most favourable aspect, but when religious hatred and oppression were infused into the bitter cup of social degradation, the draught must be one of veriest wormwood. The grown up man, accustomed to labour from his childhood, may, in many cases, have struggled firmly and devotedly against the horrors of his lot, but for the young and helpless female, how awful must have been the fate, and how degrading the doom that was in store. It was to rescue such, from the evils of their condition, that St. Peter Nolasco, and his associates united themselves into a religious institute. Among their most earnest friends and patrons, they had the honour of numbering a Spanish king, the noble hearted James of Arragon

To his munificence they were indebted for a fine convent in Barcelona. To the three ordinary vows of a monastic life, they added a fourth of collecting money for the purchase of Christians who had been taken captives by the Moors, of negotiating in person for their redemption, and whenever they had not the means of redemption, and that they discovered that the spiritual welfare of the Christian would be imperilled by his continuance in slavery, they were bound to offer some one of their own order as a substitute in his place, who was to take his chains upon him, and remain in bondage until the means of his redemption could be found.

In the course of time the diminution of slavery, arising from the declining power of the Moors, and the altered political condition of Europe led to great modification of the objects of this institute, and the holy and devoted men who followed the rule originally drawn up by its founder, were obliged to devote their lives and services to the wants of their brethren at home, and to the alleviation of the many sufferings that were to be endured by the poorer members of the Christian community.

It was the title of this heroic and meritorious institute that was adopted by Miss M'Auley for her young congregation, but she looked elsewhere for the constitutions that were to form the Charter of their religious incorporation.

It was deemed advisable to adopt measures without delay for introducing among her companions the observances of the religious state, and preparing them for the new rule of life which they were about to embrace. One way of effecting this object was to procure from some other religious house, a few nuns already professed, who, by residing for a time in the establishment in Baggot-street, would teach its inmates the ordinary religious observances, and train them to the habits of a Conventual life. When this object was attained, they would be at liberty to return to the community to which they originally belonged. Another method equally effectual, would be, to send a few of the young aspirants after religious perfection, to spend their noviciate in some convent, who, after their return, would give to the remaining sisters the benefit of their experience, and prepare them also for their religious profession.

Both methods were proposed to Miss M'Auley by the Archbishop, and she, without any hesitation, preferred the latter.

The necessary permission was procured from the Holy See, and after three months probation Miss M'Auley, Miss Doyle, and Miss Harley, received the religious habit in the Presentation Convent, George's-hill, in the month of December, 1829. At the expiration of a year, they were admitted to their religious profession and made the usual vows of poverty, chastity, and obedience, to which they added a fourth, of devoting themselves during the remainder of their lives to the service and instruction of the poor, sick, and ignorant.

Miss M'Auley and her two associates, having made their religious profession, returned to Baggot-street, in December, 1830. In the January of the following year she gave the religious habit to the sisters who had been conducting the establishment in her absence. These were six in number; namely, Sister Mary Francis Warde, Sister Mary Angela Dunne, Sister Mary De Pazzi Delany, Sister Mary Clare Moore, Sister Magdalen Flynn, and Sister Mary Teresa M'Auley.

The last-named was her niece. She had adhered to her aunt in her various struggles, taken a part in her works of charity, embraced the Catholic faith, and finally resolved on devoting herself and her talents to the glory of God and the interests of religion, in the new congregation, which her aunt had founded.

The young community had soon the pain of losing one of its most valued and useful members—Miss Elizabeth Harley, one of the three that had professed in George's-hill. During her noviciate she had suffered much from illness; but her fervent spirit either concealed or disregarded the sufferings under which she laboured. She neither omitted any of her duties, nor sought any relaxation from her severe and trying occupations. Shortly after her profession, the disease, that had been working its way

in secrecy and silence, developed itself in a manner that admitted
of no concealment, and that, alas, also bade defiance to any
remedy.   It was a confirmed and rapid consumption—that
insiduous enemy, before which so much of youthful promise has
fallen, like the sweet flowers of summer before the relentless
mower's scythe, and which spares neither youth nor beauty,
neither father's hope nor mother's pride, neither the bright eye
of genius nor the soft cheek of budding loveliness, in the indis-
criminating severity of its visitation.   This insidious enemy had
already marked poor Miss Elizabeth Harley as its victim, and
neither the skill of the physician nor the tears and prayers of an
afflicted and affectionate sisterhood could check the rapid progress of the disease.

It were needless now to tell what visions of future usefulness,
what schemes of active benevolence, what plans of alleviating
the distresses of others, or of promoting the divine glory, may
have passed through her mind, and been longed for with all the
aspirations of a most zealous and devoted heart.   They were
but the fragrance of the blossom that never is to ripen into fruit,
for death came soon and speedy, and laid her in her grave, in
the first year of her religious profession.   Nor was she the only
one who died young.   Whether it was that God wished to try
the young community in the hard ordeal of tribulation, or that
he wished to reward a devotedness so perfect and a charity so
ardent as theirs by a speedy admission to the promised crown,
it would be hard to say; but it is a singular circumstance, attend-
ing·the commencement of the Order, that, for the first six years,
no fewer than fifteen members of the Sisterhood of Mercy were
struck down by death, and passed, in the very freshness and
vigour of their youth, and the prime of their usefulness, to the
possession of that crown, which has been promised to those who
leave father, and mother, and brother, and sister, and lands, to
take their Divine Master as the portion of their inheritance.
Not one of the fifteen had reached her twenty-third year.

On the 2nd of January, 1832, the first ceremony of profession took place in the new Convent of Mercy, when five of those who had received the religious dress the preceding year made their vows, and became members of the institute. The sixth was Miss M'Auley's niece, Sister Mary Teresa. For some time past her health had been extremely precarious. Though her constitution was naturally delicate, her ardent disposition very often led her to pay but little attention to the suggestions of prudence, and to make exertions which a due regard for the delicacy of her constitution should have deterred her from making. Her aunt was often obliged to exert her influence, and make her moderate both her austerities and her labours. To her timid and sensitive conscience the necessity that arose for this exercise of authority seemed an indication from God that she was not called to the state of life in which she was then engaged, for she thought that if she was not able to do all that her charity and devotion would prompt her to do, or all that she saw others doing, she could not be chosen by Divine Providence to form one of their number. Her aunt—who had ever watched over her with the tenderest solicitude, and who knew how zealously and sincerely she was devoted to the service of the poor, and with what single-mindedness she had ever co-operated in all her plans for their welfare—endeavoured, from time to time, to remove these erroneous impressions, but in vain. They were ever and anon presenting themselves to her mind. At one period she imagined that her incapacity for the active duties of the Institute of Mercy was, as it were, a warning from Heaven to devote herself exclusively to the spirit of pious con-templation, and, for the better attainment of that object, to become a member of the Order of the Carmelites. While in this state of hesitation and uncertainty, praying for grace to know the Divine will in her regard, and, like Saul at the gate of Damascus, exclaiming, in the sincerity of her heart, " Lord, what wilt thou have me to do?" the Archbishop was brought, on important business, to the Convent. Her aunt, wishing to avail herself of such an opportunity, and having full confidence in his wisdom, requested an interview for her niece. The latter then made known to him her anxieties—both what she wished to do, and what she believed herself capable of doing. His Grace heard her with kindness, pointed out to her the advantages and merits to herself and others of the state of life in which she was already engaged, assured her that the Almighty only required what her strength and constitution enabled her to do, and that without some stronger indication of the Divine will in her regard than what she had already received, it would be rash and insecure for her to turn aside after once she had put her hand to the plough.

In this interview her doubts and fears were altogether removed. Her health, indeed, each day became more and more feeble; but each day also her life became more and more saintly and edifying to the community. Of herself she scarcely seemed to take any heed, but all her solicitude was directed to the wants of others. If she ever thought or spoke of herself, it was but to say how unworthy she was of the happiness she enjoyed. One morning, walking in the garden of the Convent, she happened to see one of the poor children of the establishment on the top of a shed, to which she had climbed with childish carelessness, and from which she was each moment in the most imminent danger of falling. In the excess of her anxiety for the poor child's safety, she screamed out to her to take care, and in the effort burst a blood-vessel in the lungs. This accident brought with it serious and alarming consequences. Consumption set in, and made rapid strides. When her recovery became hopeless, she was permitted, as is customary in similar instances, to make her profession upon her dying bed, and after receiving the last sacraments, she requested the superioress to summon the Sisters to her bedside, that, individually and in person, she may ask pardon of them for any disedification which she said she might have ever given them.

On the morning of the day of which she died, a physician, who had known her from infancy, was sitting beside her, and she asked him how many hours he thought she should live. He was moved to tears and gave an evasive answer to the question. Perceiving his unwillingness to tell her, she said: " You need not fear to tell me. People in the world are terrified at the approach of death, but a religious rejoices and sees in it an end of banishment and a beginning of happiness. Is not this the chill of death which is on me, and which you are trying to keep off ?" This was said in reference to some hot flannels in which the doctor ordered her to be wrapped, and of which she conjectured the cause. He was at length, compelled to declare that he thought she would not survive the night, which was approaching. He was right. Before morning she was dead.

Some short time after this event, Miss M'Auley's second niece, Catherine, expressed her intention of becoming a member of the Institute of Mercy. She had been educated in the convent from her youth, under the care of her aunt, and when she arrived at an age to enable her to decide on the choice of a state of life, proved herself animated with the same heroic and generous charity of which her aunt had given her so noble an example. She wished to devote herself entirely and for ever to those works of mercy to the suffering poor, which, from her earliest years she had seen performed by the edifying community in which she lived. But some obstacles were, at first, thrown in her way. Her uncle, who was one of her guardians, not appreciating the excellence of her vocation, or perhaps wishing to try still further the sincerity of her resolution, insisted on her spending at least a year in his own house. He hoped, or perhaps expected, that estrangement from the scenes and companions to which she had been so long accustomed, and the attractions of the gay world with which she would become acquainted would produce a change in her views, and induce her to abandon a determination which, in his opinion, was adopted under the impulse of an unreflecting enthusiasm; but neither the persuasions of her uncle, nor the attractions of the society, to which he took care to introduce her, could induce her to change her original intention.

God had called her and she proved herself faithful to his inspirations, and though her vocation was tried and examined, its sincerity remained unshaken in the ordeal to which it was exposed.
After some time her uncle, seeing that her mind remained unaltered, left her at liberty to follow her own wishes, when she
immediately returned to her former abode in Baggot-street, and
received the habit of the Sisters of Mercy. In due time she was
also admitted to the religious profession, and became to her
attached sisterhood a model of the most devoted charity, and the
most fervent and exact religious observance. Her great delight
was to teach and provide for the poor children in the school,
and the orphans that were inmates of the house. To perform,
with her own hands, those kind offices, which, though little in
themselves, and, perhaps, scarcely deserving of being thus mentioned, were yet, proofs of a generous and affectionate heart, and
a soul overflowing with charity. Her career promised to be
one of great virtue, and great usefulness. But, alas! Sister
Mary Agnes (for so she was called in religion), had inherited the
constitutional malady of her family. Consumption soon developed itself in her delicate frame, and after some months of suffering she also was laid by her sister's side in the cemetery of the
convent. Those who had the happiness of being associated with
her in the performance of her duties, as members of the sisterhood, long preserved the recollection of her worth, and still
speak of her with the most affectionate remembrance. But truly
afflicting to the aunt, must have been the loss of those whose
childhood she had watched over with a mother's care and to whom
she was attached with all a mother's tenderness and affection.

The good effected by the New Order of Mercy in Baggot-
street, the zeal and piety of its members, and the services it
was rendering to the ignorant, and the destitute in Dublin, began
to attract the attention and admiration of the public, not only in
the city, which was the theatre of its usefulness, but of the
kingdom at large. Applications for branch houses were made
from other localities, and the necessity of providing for these

was an additional source of care and anxiety to the foundress. So early as the year 1835 (only four years from the foundation of the Order), a convent was established in Tullamore, of which Mother Mary Anne Doyle was appointed superioress. Miss M'Auley accompanied the sisters to their new place of residence, and after a stay of some months, during which she made all the necessary arrangements for their future comfort and efficiency, she returned to Baggot-street. In the following year she established a convent of her Order in Charleville, in the County of Cork, over which she placed Mrs. Angela Dunne.

In the year 1837, she acceded to the request of the Right Rev. Dr. Nolan, Roman Catholic Bishop of Kildare and Leighlin, and sent some sisters under the care of Mrs. Mary Francis Warde, to found a convent in the town of Carlow. Application now became very numerous, for in the same year another branch of the order was established in the city of Cork, at the head of which she placed Mrs. Clare Moore, and in 1838, one in Limerick, over which Mrs. Elizabeth Moore was appointed. In May, 1840, the order was extended to Galway, and in the same year to Birr, in the King's County. Mrs. Teresa White was appointed Superioress of the one, and Mrs. Aloysius Scott of the other.

In the year 1841, the Order was extended to England, and a convent erected in the town of Birmingham. It was the last which Miss M'Auley herself was permitted by Providence to be the instrument of founding. The many cares and troubles attending the foundation of these houses; the many journeys which she was necessarily compelled to take, and the anxiety of providing all things suitable for the efficient working of every one of the several communities, were enough to break down a constitution even much stronger than hers. On her return from Birmingham, it was evident, from the great debility and exhaustion under which she was labouring, that the term of her usefulness on earth was nearly drawing to a close. After struggling with her increasing infirmity for some time. she was, at length, obliged to confine herself to her room. She wished to continue still to encourage her spiritual daughters, by her example, to the punctual fulfilment of their meritorious duties; but her divine Master showed that such was not His will, by depriving her of the power of performing them. But her patience and submission under suffering, her resignation to the divine Will at the approach of death, was most edifying and instructive. Much solicitude it was natural she should feel for the future welfare of the Order, which sprung into existence under her maternal care; and many an anxious thought she must have entertained, and given ex-pression to, about its future progress. Yet she knew that she had been but an instrument in the hands of God; and if He called her away ere half her work was done, or her contem-plated scheme of usefulness brought to a successful termination, He would Himself protect what He had created, direct it by His presiding Spirit, and make it the instrument of virtue and happiness to future generations. Much of this good she wished to be permitted to see. Many a long year she would be content to labour; and however ardent may have been her desire to be dissolved and be with God, she would yet willingly stay to be of use to her suffering brethren. But it was not thus that God, in His all-wise providence disposed. Her good works were full: she had laboured well and faithfully in the vineyard, and the Master of that vineyard was now about to confer upon her the rich and abundant reward of her devotion and fidelity. Her debility and exhaustion were very great in the last stages of her illness, but she does not seem to have suffered any considerable pain; and she often said to the sisters that were in attendance by her bedside "Oh! if this be death, it is, indeed, very easy. The Almighty has spared me very much." She preserved her faculties unimpaired to the last. A short time before her death, she had the satis-faction of hearing, that her Rule and Order were confirmed by the Holy See. The approval thereof, in 1831, was only provisional, and subject to withdrawal or ratification, as after events, or subsequent experience might render advisable. But when an experience of ten years gave additional and convincing proof of its utility, and when several prelates bore willing and honourable testimony to its merits, a second application was made by the zealous foundress, in a letter which stated her views and intentions in detail, and an express and formal approval and ratification was given by the Holy See in a rescript, bearing date the 5th July, 1841.

After the death of Miss M'Auley, in 1841, the Order of Mercy continued rapidly and widely to extend. Applications were made not only from England, but also from several of the Colonies. Branches have been astablished in the United States, and even in the remote regions of Australia. A complete list of the Convents of Mercy will be found in the appendix at the end of this work.

SISTERS OF CHARITY.

THE only other order of nuns in this country that devotes itself to the visitation of the sick in their own houses, and to the spiritual and corporal works of mercy, is that of the Sisters of Charity, established by Mrs. Mary Aikenhead, in the year 1815.

Mary Aikenhead was born in the city of Cork, about the year 1786. Her father, David Aikenhead, was a native of Scotland, and a member of the medical profession. He was a Protestant, and brought up his daughter in that persuasion. She was fifteen years old before she became a Catholic. This happy change was principally brought about by the exertions of her aunt, a Mrs. Gorman, to whose care she was confided about that period of her life. She had the happiness of enjoying the friendship of the Right Rev. Dr. M'Carthy, Coadjutor

Bishop of Cork, whose advice and encouragement tended, in a high degree, to direct her young and energetic mind to those charitable objects to which it was afterwards so successfully devoted. Some short time after the death of the Right Rev. Dr. M'Carthy she removed to Dublin, and resolving to devote herself entirely to the service of God and of the poor, and knowing that this could only be done in a proper manner by some form of a religious community, she determined to establish one for that purpose.

With one companion, who shared in her sentiments, and re-solved to share in her labours, she repaired to a Convent of the Ladies of Charity, in the Middle Gate Bar, in York, to learn the practices of a religious life, and prepare for her future mission of charity.

On the 22nd of August, 1815, she returned from York, after having made her religious profession. Immediately on her arrival in Dublin she took charge of an Orphanage, in North William-street, which was willingly entrusted to her, and which continued under her management until the removal of the com-munity to Upper Gardiner-street, in 1830, when it was committed to other hands.

In the year 1819, she made her first foundation in Stanhope-street, where she established a training school for young girls of good character, who wished to be employed as servants. This institution still exists in a flourishing condition, and contains seventy inmates, who, after being instructed in the principles of religion, and in such branches of household industry as they may subsequently require, are provided with situations, in which they earn a decent livelihood.

In the year 1826 five members repaired to Cork to establish a foundation in that city. After some time they succeeded in obtaining a most eligible site, on which they have erected a handsome and commodious building. The care of the Mag-dalen Asylum, which adjoins the convent, is committed to them, and this old and declining institution has been not only rebuilt and remodelled by them, but also placed on a footing of enlarged efficiency, and is now one of the finest institutions of its class in this kingdom.

Mrs. Aikenhead had the satisfaction of finding that her labours were appreciated by the Catholic public, and, above all, by her ecclesiastical superiors. The late Archbishop Murray procured a confirmation of the institute from the Holy See, and convents were gradually extended to Sandymount, in 1830, and to Donnybrook, in 1835. The former of these was for the visitation of the sick, and the instruction of the poor. The latter was for the reformation of poor penitent females, and was removed from Townsend-street, where it had been under their care since the year 1832.

Notwithstanding the many hospitals for the sick which Dublin can boast of, and the eminent medical institutions which it possesses, a great want was felt by the Catholic community in not having some hospital where their sick poor would receive, not only medical advice and assistance, but also that charity which religion alone inspires.

The Good Samaritan could only pour oil and wine into the wounds of the body, but a higher benevolence was wanting to minister to the mind diseased and pour balm on the more serious maladies of the soul.

Religion, like a Guardian Angel, should keep watch over the sick bed, to mitigate its sufferings during the progress of disease, and when that disease has baffled human skill and triumphed over medical power, should soothe the sorrows of the dying hour, and whisper the glad tidings of a better land in the dread moment of its dissolution. Every one that has travelled on the Continent has been struck with the order, cleanliness, and eminently religious spirit which distinguish the many hospitals which are administered by religious communities, especially those of the Sisters of Charity in France. Mrs Aikenhead was encouraged to establish such an institution in Dublin. A large house, once the town residence of the Earl of Meath, in Stephen's-green, was taken and a beginning was made. It was opened for the reception of patients on the 23rd January, 1834. The public soon discovered its value, and the poor began to feel the many blessings which it is capable of conferring, and it has from the very commencement, enjoyed a high place in the esteem and confidence, not only of the Catholic body, but of the people at large. A large addition was made in 1841, when the adjoining house, once the residence of Lord Westmeath, was rented, and the entire now forms one magnificent hospital under the name and patronage of " St. Vincent de Paul."

Their other foundations in Ireland are those of Waterford, in 1842, for the instruction of poor children and the visitation of the sick; of Claren Bridge, near Oranmore, endowed by Mrs. Redington, in 1844, who gave a house and seven acres of land for ever; of Clonmel, in 1845; and finally, of Harold's Cross, near Dublin, where the central noviciate of the Sisters of Charity has been established. In the other religious Orders of nuns in Ireland, each Convent has its own noviciate, where the young members are trained to the duties of the religious life under those of the members of the community with whom they are to be subsequently associated; but in the Order founded by Mrs. Aikenhead all the novices are trained in one central house, and formed for the due discharge of their obligations by the one individual, and under one system of direction.

Mrs. Aikenhead was confined to her room for several years before her death by the pressure of infirmity, but her active and vigorous mind retained its energy to the last, and from her bed she was able to direct the varied and complicated details of her convents in their several localities. She lived to find them increasing in numbers and in usefulness every year. Though not as widely or as numerously diffused as the convents of other Orders, yet each house established by her has, by the great ability and good management of its members, won for itself a high rank in whatever department of charity it has undertaken. Her declining years were comforted with every care and attention that her admiring daughters in religion could bestow; and, full of years and virtue, she departed this life on the 23rd day of July, 1858, at the age of seventy-two.

Her remains were conveyed to the cemetery of St. Mary Magdalen's Asylum, Donnybrook, and interred there with the usual solemn obsequies of religion, and with every tribute of respect and veneration which the Catholic people owed to her, who was the instrument, in the hands of God, of conferring such blessings on the poor of this country.

The name which the Sisters of Charity have adopted is that bestowed by the celebrated Saint Vincent de Paul on the community of religious women who devoted themselves, under his direction, to the care of the sick in Paris, and which has been since so widely diffused over France; but the Irish nuns and those of France are not in any manner connected with one another, beyond having the same name, the same patron, and having very nearly, if not exactly, the same objects of Christian charity in view.

The two Orders of "Charity" and "Mercy" resemble each other so much in their external character, that many, who are only superficially acquainted with them, believe them to be identical, while, in truth, they are perfectly distinct from one another.

In the Order of Charity the principle of centralization is strongly manifested. Its supreme authority is vested in one head. The Superioress in Dublin, or wherever she may reside, has jurisdiction over all the convents and members of the Order in Ireland. She can remove a member from one convent to another. It is her duty to see that each house has, as far as possible, a sufficient number of members, and also sufficient means of support. There is also, as we have seen, but one house where novices are trained for the Order, who, after making their profession, are sent, as may be required, to the several convents throughout the kingdom. The bishop of the diocese in which any convent out of Dublin is situated, has no immediate or direct control over its internal management.

The Order of Mercy is constituted on a totally different principle. Each convent, with only a few unimportant exceptions, is completely independent of every other. It is a perfect institution in itself. It has its own superior and its own noviciate. It is subject to the ecclesiastical jurisdiction of the bishop in whose diocese it is situated. No member of the convent can be removed to another without his consent. It may receive novices and found other convents of the Order without reference to any other persons than the bishops immediately concerned. Their constitution partakes very much of a municipal character, and the only link that binds them together is the memory of a common origin, the observance of a common rule, and the pursuit of the same great objects. We may add that in each Convent of Mercy the members are generally natives of the neighbouring town or country. The objects of their charity are the poor, sick, and ignorant of the place, which they have been acquainted with from infancy; and, after their own lives of holy labour are terminated, they are laid in their last resting-place, within a short distance of the spot where the years of their childhood were passed, and near the very parish church in which they were first admitted to the participation of those sacraments which formed the strength and consolation of their after lives.

Notwithstanding the many exceptions that must take place, especially in infant establishments, this must be the prevailing characteristic of the Institute of Mercy, and this will always give it a strong claim on the esteem and veneration of every place where it is established.

These are great advantages; but the Sisters of Charity have great and decided advantages also on their side, in the superior energy of their organization. A central authority, having power to command the services of those whom it deems most suitable to the work required, and able to concentrate its full strength on whatever object it desires to accomplish, is an advantage that

will weigh against many others.   In whose favour the balance
inclines it is not for us to say, and indeed it may not be possible
to decide; but this is quite certain, that both the Sisters of
Charity and Mercy are noble institutions, an honour to our native
land, and agents of great blessings to the best interests of religion.
We hope that for many a year it may be difficult to decide which
is the best, the most useful, or the most meritorious; and that
both may continue that heroic mission to which they have devoted themselves in generous emulation of each other's excellence, each striving to outdo the other in zeal for God's glory,
and the welfare, spiritual and temporal, of His people.

LORETTO NUNS.

IN the southern vicinity of Dublin, the house and demesne of
Rathfarnham, adjacent to the small village of that name, have
long been admired by those who have extended their walks in
'that direction, for their quiet seclusion and picturesque beauty.
The mansion itself, is one of that class of stately red brick edi-
fices which were erected about the beginning of the last century,
either by the landed proprietors, who felt themselves perfectly
at ease, on the establishment of the Hanoverian dynasty on the
throne of these realms; or by the high judicial functionaries who
occupied the places of trust and emolument at the disposal of
the government.   Much of the material of which Rathfarnham
House is built, was brought at great expense from abroad, and
its appearance and internal arrangements are in the old baronial
style of magnificence, which was usual at that period.   About
the close of the last century, and in that style of social life which

prevailed in the metropolis, as described in the pages of Sir Jonah Barrington, it became the scene of those festive meetings, which the Monks of the Screw were wont to hold before teetotalism was heard of, and the rustic arbour is still preserved and shewn, where, away from the noise of the busy and prying world, the earnest and devoted members of that illustrious fraternity, were accustomed to protract, to a late hour, their devotions to the rosy divinity that was the object of their worship. The fountain is also near at hand, whose fresh and sparkling waters gushing from a perennial spring, were used to cool—not the burning lips of the votaries who frequented the spot—but the red wine which they employed in their libations. The deities of the old mythology presided fittingly over scenes of revelling which would have better become a heathen than a Christian land, and their statues stood under the spreading oaks or towering elms that beautified the landscape. The statues have long since been removed, but the elms and oaks remain. Instead of shielding from the noontide heat, the idle and thoughtless reveller, they now spread their branches over nuns and their attentive pupils, who, arranged in silent and orderly groups around them, listen to the instructive tale or the edifying lesson which is to be treasured up in their minds. On festivals the long line of a procession, in honour of our Lady, or the Patron Saint, may be seen winding its way, from altar to altar, along the hedge of laurel, or the shaded grove, with the neatly decorated banner borne in the front, and a chorus of sweet voices chanting some litany or anthem suited to the time. The old mansion, once the abode of fashion, and the scene of revelry, is now the Convent of Loretto, and is devoted to the service of God and the education of youth.

The history of the Loretto Nuns is soon and briefly told. During the continued persecution to which the Catholic religion was subjected in England, during the reign of Elizabeth and her successors, such ladies as wished to devote themselves to the service of God, by the vows of a religious life, were obliged to repair to the Continent of Europe. Many of them did so, and it is certain, that in the reign of Maximilian of Bavaria, a community of English Nuns was formed in Munich, who practised the exercises of a religious life.

Whether from a principle of pure benevolence, or to procure the means of subsistence, they devoted themselves also to the education of such children as were committed to their care. Their rule of life and the constitutions of their institute were approved by the Holy See, and formally confirmed by its supreme authority on the 13th of June, 1713, under the title of the institute of the Blessed Virgin Mary, and from this epoch the community date the origin of their institute. At this period there were only six houses of the Order. Four of these were in Germany, and two, namely Hammersmith and York in England. The latter was established by Mrs. Frances Bedingfield *alias* Long, who was sent over from the Convent of Munich for the purpose, and who purchased for the sum of £150 the plot of ground on which the convent now stands. This was on the 5th of November, 1685, and it was a curious coincidence that it should take place on the very day and probably at the very hour, that the cry of " No Popery" was resounding from one end of the kingdom to the other. The several communities acknowledged one common Superior, who at the time of the York foundation was Mrs. Maryanne Barbara Babthorp, of the Mother House of Munich. Her services in collecting the constitutions, arranging the customs, and procuring their confirmation by the Holy See, were so important, that she has been ever since honoured as their foundress by the gratitude of the Sisterhood. This authority over all the congregations and their several members, was confirmed to her by Clement the XI., and was exercised until her death in the year 1711, at the age of 64.

Long after her death, it was renewed to her successors by the illustrious Pontiff Benedict XIV., in a bull, bearing date the 30th April, 1749, and continued to be exercised by the parent house at Munich, until its final destruction on the invasion of Germany by Napoleon.

The late Archbishop Murray, wishing to afford the means of education to the young females of the better classes of society in Dublin, and knowing the great success which the convent of our Lady at York had achieved, determined to establish a branch of this institute in his own diocese. He authorized Miss Mary Teresa Ball to proceed to York, and commence her noviciate. She left Dublin on the 11th June, 1814, with a few companions, having the same end in view; and after having performed her noviciate, and made herself perfectly acquainted with the system of education, as well as the order of its religious exercises, returned on the 10th of August, 1821. She took possession of her new residence at Rathfarnham, on the 5th of November of the following year, and commenced the institution, which has since become so well known, and so deservedly celebrated, as the convent of our " Lady of Loretto." Its excellence was soon recognised by the public, and it began to spread in all directions. A branch was founded in Navan, in the year 1833. Two fine schools for day pupils were established in the city of Dublin. They soon provided a remedy for a great religious want, by affording accommodation to such ladies as wished to practise the religious exercises of retreat. It is not necessary to follow the history of its extension in minute detail. Dalkey, Gorey, Gibraltar, Clontarf, Bray, Fermoy, followed.

In the Autumn of 1841, a colony of eleven sisters went to British India, and, under the auspices of Archbishop Carew, established themselves in Calcutta, and thence, as a centre, sent forth nine or ten branches to other parts of the country.

On the 9th of June, 1845, the Right Rev. Dr. Collier conducted eight nuns of the Order, to found a convent in the Mauritius. In 1847, a colony went with the Right Rev. Dr. Power to the province of Upper Canada, where they established themselves at Toronto, and thence spread to several other places.

The object of the institute of our Lady of Loretto, is to afford to young ladies of the wealthier classes of society the advantages of an education, which may fit them for their future condition in life. The best proof that can be given of their having attained satisfactorily this most important result, is the anxiety to secure their services for their children, displayed by those parents who are competent to appreciate their usefulness.

The high position which these convents have attained among the many educational institutions of this kingdom and its dependencies, affords also most convincing proof that the pupils who have been entrusted to them have been formed to habits of sincere, and well grounded religious observance, and imbued with those cultivated tastes and intellectual acquirements, which an educated Christian woman should possess, and which alone can shed grace and happiness on her home.

The old red brick mansion, originally purchased by the Loretto Nuns, for the purpose of a convent, is now but a small part of the group of buildings devoted to that object. As the members of the community increased, additional accommodation became necessary, and dormitories, class-rooms, and other apartments, suited to their wants had to be erected. A chapel is an essential requisite in every religious house, and the chapel of Rathfarnham is worthy of the taste and magnificence displayed in the other parts of the establishment. The design and many subordinate details of the structure are peculiar as far as we have been able to discover, to the convents of this institute. A large space in the form of a Greek cross, that is, a cross having the four arms of equal length, occupies the centre of a lofty, rectangular building. The altar, containing a beautiful piece of sculpture from the chisel of Hogan, is in the middle of this space, and the several arms of the cross are so many transepts appropriated to the different branches of the community. An enclosed and covered

L

cloister runs round the entire, and communicates by convenient doors with each department, affording easy ingress and egress to them all.   The altar is thus distinctly visible to every one in the chapel, while those in each transept are isolated from the others.

The chapel occupies a large space on the ground floor, but diminishes gradually like the steps of a pyramid as it rises through the building until it terminates in a fine cupola which gives light and ventilation to the whole.   Dormitories and corridors surround it on all sides above, and from these there are windows opening into the interior, which enable invalids and others to join in the services of the community and be present at the Holy Sacrifice without inconvenience.

Externally the convent presents the appearance of a large, commodious, and stately edifice, and it is only on entering that the real nature and magnificent arrangements of the structure are discovered.   Those who have strength and nerve to ascend the roof, may command from the parapet a view of the surrounding scenery, which, for rich and varied beauty, it would be difficult to surpass in any country.

CONVENTS OF THE PRESENTATION ORDER.

Date.	Name of Convent.	Filiation.
1777	South Presentation Convent, Cork,	Mother House,
1793	Killarney,	Sth. Convent, Cork.
1794	George's Hill, Dublin,	Sth. Convent, Cork.
1799	North Convent, Cork,	Sth. Convent, Cork.
1800	Waterford,	Sth. Convent, Cork.
1800	Kilkenny,	Sth. Convent, Cork.
1807	Richmond, Dublin,	George's Hill.
1809	Tralee,	Killarney.
1809	Dungarvan,	Waterford.
1811	Carlow,	Sth. Convent, Cork.
1813	Drogheda,	George's Hill, Dublin.
1813	Carrick,	Waterford.
1813	Clonmel,	Dungarvan.
1815	Galway,	Kilkenny.
1817	Rahan, or Killina,	George's Hill.
1817	Thurles,	Clonmel & Kilkenny.
1818	Doneraile,	Sth. Convent, Cork.
1818	Wexford,	Kilkenny.
1824	Maryborough,	Carlow.
1824	Maynooth,	Richmond.
1825	Mullingar,	Richmond.
1827	Kildare,	Carlow.
1829	Castlecomer,	Kilkenny.
1829	Bandon,	Sth. Convent, Cork.
1829	Enniscorthy,	Wexford.
1829	Dingle,	Tralee.
1829	Mountcoin,	Kilkenny.
1830	Cashel,	Thurles.
1832	St. John's, Newfoundland,	
1834	Lismore,	Waterford.

Date.	Name of Convent.	Filiation.
1834	Youghal,	Doneraile.
1834	Middleton,	Nth. Convent, Cork.
1835	Tuam,	Galway.
1835	Manchester,	Clonmel.
1837	Limerick,	Sth. Convent, Cork.
1838	Milltown,	Killarney.
1838	Bagnalstown,	Maryborough.
1838	Fermoy,	Sth. Convent, Cork.
1839	Clane,	Maryborough.
1840	Caherciveen,	Dingle.
1840	Millstreet,	Killarney.
1841	Madras,	Maynooth.
1844	Listowel,	Killarney.
1846	Castleisland,	
1846	Harbor Grace,	
1852	Stradbally,	
1853	Mitchelstown,	
	Clondalkin,	
1854	Mountmellick,	
1854	Portarlington,	
1854	San Francisco,	
1861	Oranmore,	
1862	St. Mary's, Newfoundland,	
1864	Fethard,	
	Carbonur,	
	River Head,	
	Harbor Maine,	
	Fermense,	
	Ferry Head,	
1865	Placentia,	

Note.—The convent in James's-street was founded in 1807. The community removed to Richmond in 1820.

CONVENTS OF THE ORDER OF MERCY.

1831 St. Catherine's, Dublin.

1834 Kingstown.
(Given up, but again opened in 1855.)
1838 St. Anne's, Booterstown.
1854 St. Paul's Hospital, Jervis-
street.
1855 Reformatory,   Golden-
bridge.
1861 Mater Misericordiæ.

1836 St. Joseph's, Tullamore.
St. Joseph's, Charleville.
1837 St..Leo's, Carlow.
St. Marie's of the Isle, Cork.

1857 The Hospital, Cork.
1858 Passage.
1850 Mount St. Vincent.
1854 Our Lady's Abbey, Adare.
1850 St. Catherine's, Newcastle.
St. Anne's, Rathkeale.

1838 St. Mary's, Limerick.

1839 St. Mary's, Naas.
Most Holy Trinity, Ber-
mondsey.

1856 Hospital, Great Ormond-
street, London.

1840 St. Vincent's, Galway.

1845 Magdalen Asylum.
1851 Albana, Galway.

St. Michael's, Wexford.
St. John's, Birr.

1854 St. Mary's, Nenagh.

1841 St. Marie's, Birmingham.
1842 Newfoundland.
Mt. St. Mary's, Westport.
1843 St. Ethelburga's, Liverpool.

1848 St. Edward's.
1853 St. Oswald's, Lancaster.

St. Mary's, Pittsburgh, U.S.

1846 Mount St. Vincent.
1848 Youngstown, St. Francis
Xavier.

St. Mary's, Pittsburgh, U.S.		1850	Loretto.
		1854	Holidaysbury.
Sunderland.			Darlington.
			Hexham, and
			Durham.
1844	Our Lady's, Nottingham.	1849	Clossop.
	St. Columbkille's, Kells.		
	St. Joseph's, Kinsale.		
	St. Edward's, Blandford-square.		
	H. Cross, Killarney.	1854	St. J. Baptist's, Tralee.
1845	St. Patrick's, Mallow.		
	H. Cross, Perth.		
	St. Joseph's, Chelsea.		
1846	St. Peter's, Tuam.		
	St. Mary's, Chicago, U.S.	1853	Gallina.
	St. Catherine's, New York.		
	St. Patrick's, Sligo.		
	,, Bristol.		
1847	St. Anne's, Birmingham.		
	St. Malachy's, Dundalk.		
1848	Freemantle, transferred to Gilford, Perth.		
	St. Peter's, Londonderry.		
1849	St. Elizabeth's, Wolverhampton.		
	St. Augustine's, Cheadle.		
	St. Mary's, Glasgow.		
	St. Patrick's, N. Zealand.	1855	St. Anne's.
		1860	2nd Branch.
	St. Joseph's, Derby.	1857	Belper.
1850	St. Mary's, Queenstown.		
	St. Raphael's, Loughrea.		
	St. Teresa's, Cappoquin.		
	Arkansas, U.S.		
1851	St. Joseph's, Ballinrobe.		
	St. F. Xavier's, Providence.	1853	New Haven, Connecticut.
			Hartford, do.
		1854	S. Marie's of the Isle, Newport.
			,, Rhode Island.
	St. Gabriel's, Ballinasloe.		

All Hallows, Ballina.
1852 St. Mary's Vale, Oscott.
St. Michael's, Athy.
„   Brighton.
1853 St. Angela's, Castlebar.
St. Joseph's, Navan.
Baltimore, U. States.
Im. Conception, Roscom-
mon.
1854 St. Paul's, Belfast.
St. Xavier's, Ennis.
St. Joseph's, New Ross.
D. Providence, S. Francisco.   Sacramento.
„   Drogheda.
St. Gabriel's, Dungarvan.

This year closed by a Mission of 20 Sisters to the British hospitals in Scutari, Constantinople, and Ballaclava, contributed by
the Convents in Dublin, Cork, Carlow, Charleville, Bermondsey,
Kinsale, and Chelsea.

1855 St. Mary's of the Cross,
Kilrush.
St. Liguori's, Swinford.
St. J. Baptist, Alton.
M. S. Heart, Newry.
St. Bede's, Newcastle-upon-
Tyne.
Im. Conception, Clifden.
Clifford, Yorkshire.
1856 St. Augustine's, Cheadle,
transferred to Bolton.
Im. Heart of Mary, Clona-
kilty.
Im. Conception, Enniskillen.
Brooklyn, New York.
1856 Buenos, Ayres.
1857 The Annunciation, Athlone.
Im. Conception, Hull.

Im. Conception, transferred
   from Perth.
Wigton.
Gort.
Buffalo, U. States.
1858 St. Joseph's, Ardee.
    Im. Conception, Ennis-
     corthy.
    Rochester, U. States.
    St. Catherine of Sienna,
     Edinburgh.
    Dundee.
    Cincinnati, U. States.
1858 Im. Conception, Finsbury-
     square.
1859 Im. Conception, E. Road,
     London.
    St. Patrick's, Sydney.
1860 S. Heart, Skibbereen.
    Brisbane, Australia.
    Outerard.
    Bantry.
    Downpatrick.
    Manchester, N. Hampshire.
1861 Longford.
    St. Camilla's.
    Mt. Carmel, Moat.
    Abingdon.
    N. Shields.
    Philadelphia.
1862 Worcester.
    Augusta, U.S.
    Wilburne.
    Hospital, Washington, U.S.
    Beaufort, N. Carolina.
    Westport.
    Moville.
    Helena, U.S.
    New Birmingham, U.S.
    Templemore.
    St. Louis, U.S.

APPENDIX.

PROTESTANT TESTIMONY TO THE NECESSITY OF RELIGIOUS TRAINING AND ORGANIZATION FOR WORKS OF BENEVOLENCE.

" We are persuaded that there can be no greater blessing for our country, and for its many workers who do want training and system, and who want that only, than the establishment of institutions to which organization is so essential, that a sort of unwritten code of order seems to pervade their very atmosphere. It has been re-marked that while in the Crimea, our hired nurses disgraced them-selves through incompetency and disobedience, and many of our volunteer ladies were obliged to return home ill or worn out. The Sisters of Mercy and Charity held on with unflagging spirit and energy—never surprized, never put out, ready in resource, meeting all difficulties with a cheerful spirit, a superiority, owing to their previous training and experience. We find, too, Miss Parkes saying in the report of her valuable experience among her own sex : ' I have seen many highly educated and refined women in want of em-ployment during the last year, but among them not a half-a-dozen competent (even on their own conviction), to take the responsibility of management, on a large scale, such as would be involved in the matronship of female emigrant ships—the control of a wild troop of reformatory girls—or the overseership of the female wards of a workhouse. And why ? Because they have had no training. Sis-ters of Charity abroad do all these things. Our notion of them in England is chiefly connected with the field of battle, and the nursing of the poor at their own homes. But these are but a small part of their duties. They get through in separate divisions, nearly all the duties performed (or unperformed), in our workhouses. They take

M

charge of orphan and destitute children, and bring up the girls for service—they undertake the care of the aged and crippled—distribute medicines—manage in foreign cities most of the casual relief funds—undertake the training of criminal and vagrant children. All these duties require something more for their wise fulfilment than love and patience. They require energy, foresight, economy, the habit of working in concert and subordination. Accordingly, we find the women who are to fulfil them, subjected to a severe and methodical training. And we must do the same if we would have women successfully employed in works of benevolence and social economy."—*North British Review*, February 2, 1862.

THE END.